Recent Research in Psychology

J.R. Averill   G. Catlin   K.K. Chon

Rules of Hope

Springer-Verlag
New York Berlin Heidelberg
London Paris Tokyo Hong Kong

James R. Averill
Department of Psychology
University of Massachusetts at Amherst
Tobin Hall
Amherst, MA 01003, USA

George Catlin
Department of Psychology
University of Massachusetts at Amherst
Tobin Hall
Amherst, MA 01003, USA

Kyum Koo Chon
Sung Kyun Kwan University
Seoul, Korea

Averill, James R.
   Rules of hope / James R. Averill, George Catlin, Kyum Koo Chon.
      p.   cm. — (Recent research in psychology)
   Includes bibliographical references.
   ISBN 0-387-97219-6 (alk. paper)
      1. Hope—Psychological aspects. 2. Hope. I. Catlin, George.
II. Chon, Kyum Koo. III. Title. IV. Series.
BF575.H56A95   1990
152.4—dc20   89-49228

Printed on acid-free paper.

Camera-ready copy provided by the authors.
Printed and bound by Edwards Brothers, Ann Arbor, Michigan.
Printed in the United States of America.

9 8 7 6 5 4 3 2 1

ISBN 0-387-97219-6 Springer-Verlag New York Berlin Heidelberg
ISBN 3-540-97219-6 Springer Verlag Berlin Heidelberg New York

Preface

Hope is a powerful ally. In a recent presidential campaign, one candidate implored voters to "Keep hope alive!", presumably by voting for him. Ironically, the theme "Springtime of Hope" had just contributed to two straight landslide victories for his opposition.

In an entirely different field, health care providers are equally aware of the importance of hope. Hope is a sign of health, a fighting spirit, and faith that somehow good will triumph. In fact, hope is so much a part of our present cultural understanding of what it is to be a person, that when we think of someone "without hope," we imagine a person just barely on this side of the grave.

Yet what exactly is hope? How is it different from ordinary wants and desires? Under what circumstances does hope arise, and when is it lost? Is hope an emotion like anger and love, or something altogether different? And if it is an emotion, does that imply it is a universal phenomenon, or might "hope" be experienced differently in different cultures?

These are some of the questions this book sets out to answer. We draw our data from detailed inquiries into the experience of hope in two cultures (American and Korean) as well as an analysis of hope in metaphors and maxims.

Contents

Introduction:
Pandora's Legacy

Over three decades ago, during the height of the cold war, Menninger (1959) posed the question: "Are we not duty bound to speak up as scientists, not about a new rocket or a new fuel or a new bomb or a new gas, but about this ancient but rediscovered truth, the validity of Hope in human development" (p. 491). Not in response to Menninger's exhortation, but reflecting the salutary effects of hope in a variety of challenging contexts, especially recovery from illness, references to hope are now frequent in medical and psychological writings (e.g., Breznitz, 1986; Frank, 1973; Friedman, Chodoff, Mason, & Hamburg, 1963; Gottschalk, 1974; Spence, Scarborough, & Ginsberg, 1978; Snyder, 1989). The references are, however, scattered, and systematic analyses have been few (cf. Fromm, 1968; Lynch, 1965; Stotland, 1969).

What does it mean to say that a person has gained or lost hope, for example, when faced with a life-threatening illness such as cancer? This question, it will be noted, does not call for a strict or scientific definition of hope. Rather, it concerns the way people think and

1

reason about hope in everyday life, and the consequences of such thinking for their well-being. Keeping in mind this emphasis on hope as ordinarily conceived, one goal of the research reported in this book can be stated as follows: to make explicit our implicit (everyday) conception of hope, and to explore the relation of hope to social systems, on the one hand, and to individual behavior, on the other.

Another goal of the research was to use hope to explore issues relevant to theories of emotion. For the most part, our theories of emotion have been based on a rather narrow base. Fear, anger, and to a lesser extent, grief and love have been the primary emotions investigated. Yet, literally hundreds of emotions are recognized in ordinary language (Averill, 1975; Johnson-Laird & Oatley, 1989; Storm & Storm, 1987). What would our theories of emotion be like if, instead of fear and anger, we took an emotion such as hope as our paradigm case?

A critic might object at the outset that hope is not an emotion, at least not a very prototypic emotion (i.e., a state that shares the salient features of the general category, "emotion"). This is an issue about which we will have much to say later, after the presentation of Studies 1 and 2 (in Chapters 1 and 2, respectively). For the moment, it suffices to acknowledge that most contemporary theories of emotion do not include hope within their domain. That, however, may say more about the nature of our theories than about the nature of hope. Current theories of emotion are a product of a particular social-historical period; and our notions of what represents a basic or prototypic emotion are as much a reflection of our theoretical assumptions as they are of empirical discovery. There have been times past when hope was counted among the most fundamental emotions.

Historical Perspectives on Hope

The idea of hope has been a major thread running through much of the Western history; hence, hope has been the subject of many analyses of a broad philosophical or cultural nature, beginning with the ancient Greeks. Pandora, it may be recalled, was the Greek equivalent of the biblical Eve. When Prometheus stole fire from heaven and gave it to humankind, Zeus ordered that a woman be fashioned who would bring misery to the race of men. She was presented to Epimetheus (the brother of Prometheus) who, ignoring a warning not to accept any gift from the gods, took her as his wife. Pandora brought with her a box containing every human ill. When Epimetheus opened the box, all the ills escaped, save one—hope.

The tale of Pandora is ambiguous. Was hope another ill like the others that had escaped, or was it a benefactor left behind to aid humankind? The Greeks seemed ambivalent about hope; but in general they viewed it more as a bane rather than as a boon. According to Plato, for example, the mortal aspect of the soul or *psyche* is "subject to irresistible affections—first of all, pleasure, the greatest incitement to evil; then pain, which deters from good; also rashness and fear, two foolish counselors, anger hard to be appeased, and hope easily led astray" (*Timaeus*, 69d). In a similar vein, the dramatist, Euripedes, referred to hope as a "curse upon humanity" (quoted by Menninger, 1959, p. 483).

Our current conception of hope owes more to the Judeo-Christian tradition than to classical Greek thought. In fact, according to some authors (e.g., Myers, 1949), the Greek term, *elpis*, which is usually translated as "hope," actually refers to a different kind of experience. But be that as it may, the Judeo-Christian tradition treats hope as a highly valued condition. Hope is, in fact, one of the three theological virtues recognized by Christianity, the others being faith and charity or love. (A virtue may be defined as a disposition to do what is best, according to one's potential. This includes the disposition to experience relevant emotional states—in this case, hope.)

In view of the above, it is not surprising that throughout much of the medieval period hope was regarded as a fundamental emotion. This can perhaps be best illustrated by reference to the 13th century theologian, Thomas Aquinas, whose analysis and classification of the emotions remains influential even today (cf. Arnold, 1960). On the basis of criteria that need not concern us here, Aquinas (1967) distinguished eleven basic emotions; and of these eleven, four (joy, sadness, hope, and fear) were postulated as primary.

Among later, more secularly oriented writers, mention might be made of two of the British Empiricists, Hume (1739/-1888) and Hartley (1749/1966), both of whom classified hope among the fundamental emotions. Since their views were similar, only a brief summary of Hartley's classification scheme will be given here.

According to Hartley, emotions are aggregates of simple ideas, united by association. What leads a state to be classified as emotional is its relationship to pleasure and pain. Pleasure, associated with the idea of its exciting object, is *love*. When love reaches a certain degree of intensity, so that action is encouraged, we have *desire*. If the desired object is in the future and only possible, we experience *hope*. If our hope is fulfilled, the result is *joy*. When the joy is past, there remains *pleasing recollection*. These five emotions (love, desire, hope, joy, and pleasing recollection) are, on the positive side, "general passions of human nature." There is a corresponding series of five negative emotions, derivatives of pain (hate, aversion, fear, grief, and displeasing recollection or resentment).

For a somewhat different orientation, we might mention the views of Kant, one of the pivotal figures in modern philosophy. Kant was concerned primarily with the analysis of reason; his comments on the emotions are therefore somewhat superficial, unsystematic, and even contradictory, but nevertheless instructive.

In his *Anthropology* (1800/1978), Kant compared the emotions to diseases of the mind, to the extent that they are contrary to deliberate, rational thought. Hope is no exception. "The mind embraces hope as an emotion without reservation because of the unexpected emergence of a prospect of immeasurable good fortune; consequently, the emotion keeps rising until it reaches the point of suffocation" (p. 159). Elsewhere, however, Kant (1781/1966, p. 516) indicated that one of his three major critiques (namely, the *Critique of Judgment*) corresponds roughly to the question: For what may

I hope, if I do as I should? The implication seems to be that hope is like a disease if it leads one to act immorally or imprudently, but that it is good if it inspires one to lead a moral, rational life.

Kant was a leading spokesman for the Enlightenment (eighteenth and early nineteenth centuries), during which time the explicitly religious rationale for hope was gradually replaced by a different kind of faith—in progress based on reason. For the more radical advocates of enlightenment, man became God; science became religion; and hope became secularized. But man proved to be feeble and unwilling god; and the promises of science rang hollow in the sweatshops spawned by the industrial revolution. Not surprisingly, then, the Enlightenment gave way to romanticism and even nihilism. Nietzsche may be taken as representative of the latter trend. Harking back to the Greek myth, Nietzsche (1878/1986) observes that, by including hope among the evils in Pandora's box, Zeus only wanted to prevent humans from taking their own lives when overwhelmed by misfortune. Hope, Nietzsche averred, "is the worst of all evils, for it protracts the torment of man." (p. 45)[1]

This brief historical survey, cursory as it is, suffices to illustrate three important points. First, hope has occupied a prominent place within the Western cultural tradition, which fact alone would make it a worthy topic of investigation. Second, hope has often been treated as a basic or fundamental emotion, and hence its analysis can tell us something about emotions in general. And, third, our conception of hope is to a certain extent culturally relative, varying from one historical period to another.

---

[1]   Actually, Nietzsche was a reluctant nihilist at best. His later writings, expecially, had a messianic quality in which hope could find a place. Thus, his prophet Zarathustra could proclaim: "Let your love to life be love to your highest hope; and let your highest hope be the highest thought of life . . . [namely] this, man is something that is to be surpassed" (Nietzsche, 1883-1884/n.d., p. 47).   Clearly, Nietzsche was no more consistent in his attitudes toward hope than was Kant, although by extolling the passions over reason, he turned Kant on his head, so to speak.

Recent Developments

Relatively little systematic psychological research is available on hope per se (cf. Stotland, 1969; Breznitz, 1986). There is, however, a growing body of data on a related phenomenon, namely, optimism. It has been shown, for example, that people tend to recall, perceive, forecast, and interpret events in a more positive than negative fashion (for general reviews, see Matlin & Stang, 1979; Taylor & Brown, 1988), although there are large and apparently stable individual differences in this tendency (Scheier & Carver, 1985). A variety of mechanisms have been postulated to account for optimistic biases, including motivational distortion (e.g., due to the need to maintain a belief in a just world or to feelings of invulnerability) and inappropriate cognitive heuristics (e.g., failure to take into account base rates). It has also been suggested that optimistic biases have their roots in biological evolution (Tiger, 1979), and/or that they are a consequence of behavioral control mechanisms (Scheier & Carver, 1985).

Research on optimistic biases provides valuable insights into why people often remain hopeful in the face of adversity; however, it does very little to clarify the nature of hope qua emotion. Hope is not simply a species of optimism. For example, a person can meaningfully say, "I am very pessimistic, but nevertheless hopeful." Indeed, one can sometimes be so pessimistic that "there is nothing left but hope." We will have much more to say about the distinction between hope and optimism in chapter 5. For the moment, suffice it to note that conceptually hope is more closely related to fear than to optimism.

Although psychological studies of hope are relatively rare, there is a large modern-day philosophical/theological literature on hope (e.g., Capps, 1970; Godfrey, 1987; Marcel, 1951), and also a nascent body of sociological research (e.g., Desroche, 1979). Hope also plays a prominent role in many socio-political movements, secular as well as theological.

Marxism is a notable example (Bloch, 1959/1986)); so, too, is "Americanism" (Bellah, 1967).

Between the detailed social-psychological research on possible mechanisms mediating optimistic biases in information processing and the more global sociological and philosophical literature on hope, there lies a vast ground that has been relatively unexplored. That is the ground occupied by most people who apply their intuitive and implicit theories of hope in the conduct of their daily lives. That is also the ground explored by the present research.

An Overview of the Studies

The results of four studies are reported in Chapters 1 through 4, respectively. Studies 1 and 2 explored by means of questionnaire the way people experience and interpret representative episodes of hope. The same questionnaire and subjects were used in both of these initial studies, but the goals were different. Study 1 focused on the social norms or rules that help constitute and regulate hope, whereas Study 2 examined the similarities and differences between hope and other emotions, such as anger and love. Study 3 tested the generality of the results of the first two studies through an analysis of metaphors of hope, as found in folk sayings, maxims, and everyday slang expressions. Finally, Study 4 compared hope in two different cultures, the United States and Korea.

Although the studies are largely descriptive, they do not proceed without theoretical preconception, and that preconception should be made explicit at the outset. Ours is a social-constructionist view of emotion (Averill, 1980a, 1980b, 1982, in press a). Stated most generally, emotions are conceived of as syndromes or systems of behavior that comprise the appraisal of situations, patterns of response, and the selfmonitoring (interpretation) of behavior. According to many traditional theories, emotions are hard-wired into the nervous system during the course of evolution, i.e., they represent innate affect programs (Izard, 1977; Tomkins, 1981). Other theories (e.g., Mandler, 1984; Schachter, 1971) treat the emotions as undifferentiated states of physiological arousal, given form or meaning by the person's interpretation of the situation.

From a social-constructionist point of view, emotions are structured according to social norms or rules. During the process of socialization the child (or adult) learns that under certain circumstances, certain kinds of appraisals and responses (including subjective experiences) are appropriate. These psychological syndromes are products of the prevailing needs of the society and views of the nature and role of the individual. To the extent that societies differ in their needs and understandings of the individual, the social constructionist perspective predicts differences in the experience of emotions, and that is a good part of the reason for our comparison of Korean and American hopes in Study 4. Needless to say, within any given society considerable slippage may occur during socialization, so that no two individuals will have the same internal representation of the relevant rules. Hence, no two persons will experience and express an emotion in exactly the same way. Our concern is not, however, with such individual differences. Rather, our concern is with the general cultural model ("implicit theory") from which such individual differences are derived. In the next chapter, we begin this investigation by exploring the extent to which specific rules of hope can be identified within the current American culture.

I

Study 1:
The Anatomy of Hope

To the child who knows nothing of anatomy, the inside of a human body is probably construed as a relatively undifferentiated soft mass. The prevailing popular view of emotions is not too different from this. Emotions are viewed as vague, ineffable, and only describable through metaphor. Some psychological theories are little different. The structure of emotion is often attributed to cognitive variables whereas the feeling tone or *qualia* is contributed by undifferentiated arousal. From a social constructionist perspective, emotions have an internal structure—an anatomy, so to speak. Biologically oriented theories share this assumption. As the name implies, however, a social constructionist position attributes the "anatomy" of emotion to social norms or rules, not information encoded in the genes. The purpose of Study 1, therefore, was to identify the rules that help constitute hope for Americans today.

Two characteristics of norms assist their identification. First, norms produce regularities in behavior; and, second, sanctions ensue if norms are violated. Correspondingly, Study

1 was designed to identify regularities in the everyday experience of hope (e.g., as manifested in representative episodes), and to explore the conditions under which hope is considered inappropriate (e.g., when the rules of hope are violated).

With respect to methodology, Study 1 involved detailed written questionnaires. The limitations and advantages of self-reports have been the topic of frequent debate, the details of which need not concern us here. Suffice it to say that we agree with Harré (1983) when he observes "that the structure of ordinary language reflects and in part creates the psychology of the people who use that language, through the embedding of implicit theories in terms of which experience is organized" (p. 54). Specifically, with regard to the present research, our primary focus was on the implicit theories that people use when reasoning about hope in everyday affairs. From this perspective, we are more concerned with how people *believe* they should behave (the rules of hope) than with how they actually do behave on any particular occasion. Of course, we assume that on the average, or over the long run, people conform their behavior to social rules, as they conceive those rules to be.

Methods

Subjects

Subjects were recruited from undergraduate psychology courses at the University of Massachusetts, Amherst. They received course credit for participation. Testing continued until a total of 150 subjects (48 males and 102 females) completed usable questionnaires. Ages ranged from 17 to 37 years, with a mean of 19.6. Approximately half of the subjects (51%) were freshmen; the remainder were distributed about evenly among sophomores, juniors, and seniors. Preliminary statistical analyses and comparisons of open-ended responses revealed no consistent or reliable differences as a function of gender or grade level. Hence, these variables are ignored in the presentation of the results.

The Questionnaire

The questionnaire consisted of a mixture of objective questions (rating scales, multiple-choice items, etc.) and open-ended questions. (See Appendix.) The objective questions were based on extensive pilot testing, so that they included the most common responses made to a given question as well as other logical alternatives. Thus, the choices provided by the questionnaire represented the full range of responses to each item. This point merits emphasis because the purpose of the study was to explore the *popular* conception of hope, not to confirm or reject any theories the authors might hold. For each objective question, space was also provided for responses other than those delineated on the questionnaire, and, whenever appropriate, subjects were asked to explain their objective responses in an open-ended fashion.

The initial part of the questionnaire sought to distinguish hope from simple wants and desires. The second and largest part of the questionnaire pertained to a representative episode of hope experienced during the past year. The items of this part covered such issues as: the event hoped for and how it was appraised (e.g., in terms of importance and probability of occurrence); conditions that initiated and terminated the episode; changes in affect and behavior while hoping; and retrospective evaluations of the episode as favorable or unfavorable. A third part of the questionnaire explored "forbidden hopes"; that is, events that would make life easier or more enjoyable but that are not appropriate objects of hope. A final part of the questionnaire concerned the nature of hope as an emotion; responses to this last part constitute Study 2, discussed in Chapter 2.

Procedure

Questionnaires were administered in small groups, typically 10 to 15 subjects at a time. As subjects arrived they were given the questionnaire, which contained all necessary written instructions. Most subjects required 40 minutes to an hour to complete the questionnaire.

The results will be presented in roughly the order that the items appeared in the questionnaire. This provides a sense of how subjects saw the items as they worked through the questionnaire. It also allows a convenient division of the results into three parts. The first part clarifies what it means to hope for something, as opposed to simply wanting or desiring something; the second part presents normative data on representative episodes of hope; and the third part explores the conditions under which hope is inappropriate. From these data we infer, in the final section of the chapter, the general principles or social rules that help constitute the everyday experience and expression of hope.

Distinguishing Hope from Want and Desire

The first three items of the questionnaire asked subjects to describe (a) something they presently *want* or *desire* very much, but they do *not* hope for; (b) something they not only want, but also hope for; and (c) the features present in the second episode, that make it an instance of hope and not simply wanting.

The purpose of these items was methodological as well as substantive. Methodologically, they served to focus subjects' attention on hope as a unique experience, distinct from want and desire. Thus, when subsequently asked to describe a representative episode of hope, subjects would be less likely to conflate hope with other, closely related states. On a more substantive level, content analyses of these items allowed a preliminary assessment of the distinguishing characteristics of hope.

Content analyses of the responses distinguishing hope from want and desire were done in the following manner. First, three judges independently sorted the responses into relatively homogeneous categories, using any criteria they thought appropriate. The categories thus derived were then consolidated, and a second sorting was made, using the combined set of categories. Following this second sorting, any category was eliminated if it contained less than 5 items, and its items were reassigned. Additional categories also were created as necessary to accommodate new groupings of items. In order to be included in a category, at least 2 of the three judges had to agree on the placement of an item. A final check was then made of the items within the categories, and any disagreements were resolved through discussion.

By far, the major feature that distinguished hope from want or desire had to do with the *probability of attainment.* Almost half the subjects said that the object of hope was either less realistic (26.7%) or more realistic (22.7%) than the object wanted. In other words, the objects of hope tend to fall in the middle range of probabilities. Among the other distinguishing features, the most prominent was *importance*-- mentioned by 12.7% of the subjects. On occasion, people may very much want something that they nevertheless regard as trivial (e.g., an ice-cream cone); by contrast, hope typically concerns matters of vital interest. The object of hope was also more likely to be described as *less materialistic* (5.3%), and as *socially more acceptable* (4.7%). For example, a person might want a good deal of money, but not hope for it because money is too materialistic; or he might desire sexual relations with a large number of women, but not hope for it because of moral considerations. Finally, subjects tended to describe the objects of hope as more *enduring and/or in the future* (4.0%), or as *more abstract and/or intangible* (3.3%), than the objects of want or desire.

From these preliminary analyses, we can already discern in broad outline three general principles or rules of hope. The first principle emphasizes prudence—hope necessarily involves some uncertainty, but people should not hope for objects that are too improbable or unrealistic. The second principle concerns the importance of the object—people should not hope for trivial events. Or, stated somewhat differently, hope has priority in the hierarchy of a person's wants and desires. The third principle reflects moral values—people should not hope for objects that are socially unacceptable.

This third principle deserves additional comment. In contemporary American society, much is oriented around personal, material gain, a fact that was reflected in the wants and desires that subjects expressed; yet, such individualistic pursuits are bounded by the ideals of public morality. The principle that people should not hope for objects that are socially unacceptable implies that some understanding of public morality can be had through analysis of appropriate objects of hope, a point to which we will return in Chapter 4 when we compare American and Korean hopes.

It might also be noted that the distinguishing features embodied in the above three principles focus primarily on the objects of hope (e.g., their likelihood, importance, moral value, time of occurrence, and abstractness) as opposed to the behavior of the individual. The distinction between hope and want evidently is not based on specific responses; people may behave in much the same way whether they hope for or merely want something. As we shall see below, however, hope is related to action tendencies in a way that want or desire is not.

Representative Episodes of Hope

In order to explore in depth the normative aspects of hope, the bulk of the questionnaire was devoted to a detailed description of a representative episode. Subjects were asked to think back over the previous year and pick an episode that met the following two conditions: (a) It represented hope, not simply want or desire; and (b) it both *started* and *ended* within the year. The latter condition was imposed primarily to enable us to study the entire course of an episode of hope, including the terminating conditions. It also had the effect of eliminating extremely long-term and abstract hopes, such as for world peace or to be a good person. The majority of subjects (63%) chose episodes that lasted from one to six months (12% indicated a shorter, and 25% a longer duration).

The data which follow are based on subjects' descriptions of these representative episodes. We consider, first, the objects of hope, i.e., the kinds of things subjects hoped for.

Objects of Hope

Subjects first gave an open-ended description of the events they hoped for, and then they rated those events along three dimensions—probability of occurrence, importance, and personal vs situational control.

Based on the open-ended descriptions, the hoped-for events were grouped into three broad categories, plus a miscellaneous category. The largest group of subjects (n=64, 41.3%) described episodes that involved *achievement-related* goals (e.g., success in some academic, artistic, or athletic endeavor, obtaining a good job, and the like). The hopes of the second largest group (n=38, 25.3%) pertained to *interpersonal relationships*. These included both romantic hopes and hopes for good relations with roommates, families, etc. The third group (n=13, 8.7%) expressed *altruistic* hopes for the well-being of another person, such as a relative recovering from a serious illness. Finally, a miscellaneous category contained 37 subjects (24.7%) whose hopes included a diverse set of goals, from material objects (e.g., a new car) to changes in their own personalities (e.g., to become a more outgoing person).

Needless to say, there is little interest in these groups per se. A different sample of subjects in different life circumstances (e.g., community residents, senior citizens) might hope for different sorts of things. Our concern with the groupings is primarily methodological: To what extent are the results to be reported below specific to the types of events for which our particular subjects were hoping? Or, to put the question somewhat differently, to what extent can the results be generalized to other kinds of events? In answering this question, it will be helpful first to consider the way subjects evaluated the objects of their hopes along the dimensions of importance, probability of attainment, and personal vs situational control.

Importance. Subjects were asked to rate the importance of the event they hoped for on an 11-point scale ranging from 0 (not at all important) to 10 (very important). Separate ratings were made for the beginning, middle and end of the episode. The mean of these three ratings showed the most significant and stable relations with other variables; therefore, unless otherwise indicated, the "average importance" (mean of the three ratings) was employed in the analyses reported below.

The average importance score for all subjects was 8.15 (S.D.=1.70). This value is quite high, a fact that deserves some emphasis. It reinforces a point made in the previous section distinguishing hope from want and desire, namely, that people tend to hope for things they consider significant or vital to their concerns.

Probability of attainment. As with importance, subjects were asked to rate the chances that their hopes would be fulfilled for the beginning, middle and end of the episodes. The 11-point scale was expressed in percentages, with 0% representing no chance and 100% representing certainty. The mean rating of chance stayed virtually constant at 58% for the beginning, middle and end. However, the standard deviation increased from 25.5% at the beginning to 34.1% at the end ($p < .01$) as some subjects grew confident that their hopes would be fulfilled, and others realized theirs would not.

Once again the mean of the three probability scores (beginning, middle, end) showed the most stable and significant relations with other variables. Thus the average score was employed in all succeeding analyses, unless otherwise stated.

Personal vs situational control. In varying degrees, individuals are able to influence the events they hope for. To tap this dimension, subjects were asked to rate the objects of their hope on a scale ranging from "completely due to factors under your own control" (0) to "completely due to factors beyond your control" (10). The mean response was 5.23 (S.D.=2.78). The modal rating (by 32 subjects) was 5.0, the midpoint of the scale.

Differences among types of events. The above data allow us to address the question raised earlier, namely, to what extent are the specific episodes described by subjects (the details of which are presented below) representative of hope in general? Or, stated differently, to what extent can we generalize the results of this study to hope in other contexts?

As shown in Table 1.1, significant differences in levels of both importance and control were found between groups hoping for different types of events (based on analyses of variance). The subjects with altruistic hopes were most distinct in that the importance of their hopes was significantly higher than for all other groups (which did not differ among themselves). Also, altruistic hopes were characterized by a higher degree of situational as opposed to personal control over the outcome. Understandably, the group hoping for improved interpersonal relationships reported significantly more personal (as opposed to situational) control than the altruistic group, but less than those hoping for achievements. In light of the differences between groups on the dimensions of importance and personal vs situational control, the stability of the chance ratings across groups is particularly worthy of note. More than any other variable, probability of attainment may be a stable characteristic of hope.

The data presented in Table 1.1 raise the possibility that any differences observed as a function of the objects of hope (e.g., achievement vs altruistic hopes) are actually due to differences in more fundamental characteristics of the episodes (e.g., importance, personal vs situational control). To test this possibility, a series of preliminary analyses were done comparing the different groups comprising Table 1.1 on all the remaining variables to be reported below (initiating and terminating conditions, thoughts and feelings, instrumental responses, etc.—a total of 74 variables). Significant differences ($p < .05$) were observed on 33 of the variables. However, when the degree of personal control and the importance of the event were included as covariates in the analyses, the number of variables for which the groups differed significantly was reduced to 10. It is not possible to say how many of these differences might be significant by chance alone, since many of the variables were correlated. However, 10 is not much greater than would be expected by chance. This suggests that it is not the specific type of event that distin-

Table 1.1. Episodes of hope classified according to type of object, with mean ratings of the importance of the object, the subjective probability of attainment, and perceived personal versus situational control over the object.

| | Type of object | | | |
	Achievement (N=64)	Relationship (N=38)	Altruistic (N=13)	Miscellaneous (N=37)
Importance	8.26$_a$	7.51$_a$	9.92$_b$	7.99$_a$
Probability of attainment	60.2%	56.7%	59.7%	56.6%
Personal vs situational control*	4.19$_a$	5.66$_b$	9.08$_c$	5.16$_b$

Note. Scale values range from 0 to 10 (or 0% to 100%). Different subscripts indicate significant differences (p <.05) between figures within rows.

*Higher numbers indicate greater situational control.

guishes the way a person experiences hope, but rather the assessed importance of the event, and the degree of control that the person has over it.

To summarize briefly, objects of hope typically (a) touch upon a person's vital interests, (b) have a remarkably consistent, "just better than average" probability of attainment, and (c) involve some degree of personal control. Needless to say, each of these features is often violated. For example, we all hope for trivial events at times (e.g., "I hope it will be sunny tomorrow"), but that is a rather extended use of the term (analogous to, "I fear it will rain tomorrow"). Also, in the case of extremely important events, such as recovery from a terminal illness, hope is common despite objectively low probabilities and the absence of personal control. In these instances, however, the subjective appraisals of the probability and degree of personal control may nevertheless be in keeping with the norms of hope. That is, what people know to be the case on an intellectual level may be different from what they feel to be the case on a personal level.

Initiating Conditions

A list of five causal variables (changes in circumstance) that might initiate an episode of hope was compiled from pilot data. Subjects were asked to check which *one* of the five items best described the change in circumstance that initiated their episode of hope. (A sixth space was also provided for "Other" responses.) The results are shown in Table 1.2.

Table 1.2 suggests that the most common initiating conditions for hope are events that cause: (a) a decrease in the probability of a previously certain event, (b) an increase in the probability of a previously unlikely event, and/or (c) an increase in the appraised importance of an event. These results are hardly surprising in view of the findings presented earlier. That is, the object of hope is typically something important to the individual, the occurrence of which is neither too likely nor unlikely. Thus, any change in the importance or probability of an event that would bring it into the range of an appropriate object of hope might initiate an episode.

Affective Reactions During Hope

In ordinary language, the terms "feeling" and "emotion" are often used interchangeably. But what constitutes the feeling of an emotion—in this case, the feeling of hope? To address this issue, albeit in a very rough and approximate way, subjects were asked to complete a short adjective check list, once for how they felt about the object before they started hoping, and once for how they felt after the episode had begun. The items on the list consisted of 12 clusters of closely related adjectives (e.g., the three adjectives, "confident," "assured," and "optimistic" formed one cluster; "uncertain," "confused," and "bewildered" formed another). Each cluster could be rated "not at all" (0), "somewhat" (1), or "very much"

Table 1.2. Changes in circumstances that initiated episodes of hope.

Change in Circumstance	Percentage of subjects endorsing item
I was confident that the event would occur; but then I realized it was not certain, and so I started to hope.	28.0%
The event seemed far in the future; there was time to worry about it later. But as the event grew closer (became more imminent), I started to hope.	23.3%
The event seemed very unlikely; but then the chances increased, and so I started to hope.	18.7%
I had not thought about the event before; it represented a new possibility for me.	14.7%
The event seemed unimportant to me; but then I came to realize how important it actually was.	7.3%
Other[a]	8.0%

[a]Responses to the "other" category were generally variations on one or more of the given descriptions.

(2).   The mean before and after ratings are presented in Table 1.3.

Two-way analyses of variance were performed on the data, with "before" and "after" ratings representing a within-subject factor and initiating conditions representing the other, between-subject factor. With regard to the latter, four groups of subjects were formed. For example, one group consisted of those subjects (n = 42) who started to hope when they realized that the chance of attaining the event they desired

Table 1.3. Changes in affective experience from before to after subjects started to hope, and the interaction of change scores with initiating conditions.

Variable	Before	After	Change (Af-Be)	Significance of change	Interaction effects[b]
anxious, nervous, apprehensive about the future	1.25	1.28	.03		
confident, assured, optimistic	.89	1.05	.16	<.05	<.01
good, pleased, glad	.90	1.03	.13	<.05	
helpless, powerless, lacking in control	.71	.87	.16		<.05
uncertain, confused, bewildered	.95	.87	-.08		<.05
restless, tense, aroused physiologically	.76	.78	.02		
relieved, calm, satisfied	.53	.64	.11		
depressed, unhappy, sad	.57	.54	-.03		<.01
discouraged, let down, disappointed	.44	.52	.08		<.01
irritable, hostile, aggravated	.40	.48	.08		
ashamed, embarrassed, guilty	.17	.18	.01		
indifferent, not caring	.57	.16	-.41	<.01	<.05

Note.--Each cluster of adjectives was rated on a scale from 0 = not at all, 1 = somewhat, 2 = very much. Responses are rank ordered by dominant mood after hope began.

[b]See Table 2 for a description of the initiating conditions used to determine interaction effects. Subjects were assigned to four groups, based on their endorsement of items 1, 2, 3, and 5 in Table 2. Subjects endorsing item 4 ("new possibility") and item 6 ("other") were not included in the analysis. The nature of the interactions are discussed in the text.

became less certain (the first item listed in Table 1.2). Subjects were excluded from analysis if they indicated that the object of their hope was a new possibility (the fourth item in Table 1.2; n = 22), since these subjects would have no basis for making "before" ratings.   Subjects who endorsed the "other" category (n = 12) also were eliminated, since their eliciting conditions did not form a homogeneous category.

As can be seen from Table 1.3, few statistically significant changes occurred in the mean ratings (main effects) from before to after the initiation of an episode.   On the other hand, one-half the items showed significant interaction effects between changes in affective experience and initiating conditions.   Changes in a person's feelings during an episode of hope evidently depend more on the nature of the initiating circumstances than on the nature of hope per se.

The specifics of the interactions noted in Table 1.3 need not concern us here.   After the fact, most are intuitively obvious.   For example, when hope was initiated by a previously certain event becoming uncertain, self-reported affect generally changed in a negative direction (e.g., toward greater depression).   Other initiating conditions resulted either in little change, or positive changes in self-reported affect.

The frequency of interaction effects (especially as contrasted with the paucity of main effects) illustrates how misleading it can be to speak of hopeful feelings as though they formed a single affective state.   Depending on the initiating circumstances, hope may be embedded in nearly opposite overall patterns of feeling.   One person may be hopeful in the midst of anxiety over the prospect of losing something he or she expected to secure, while another's hope may be embedded in sudden optimism regarding a previously improbable event.   While a theoretical argument might be made that the hope itself—isolated from the overall emotional state—is the same in both cases, there is little empirical support for such an argument.   In daily life, one may feel hopefully—just as one may respond hopefully—in any of a variety of different (and even opposing) ways, depending on the circumstances. We would argue that the same is true of other emotions as well (e.g., anger—Averill, 1982).[1]

Instrumental Responses during Hope

We have already noted that hope, like want and desire, is not characterized by any *specific* response. What a person does when hopeful depends on the object of hope and on the specifics of the situation. Nevertheless, we have also suggested that hope is associated with action in general. We must now make that association more explicit.

From open-ended responses to pilot questionnaires, a list was compiled of seven actions that might be taken as a consequence of hope. These actions were listed on the questionnaire with the following instructions:

> The following question is hypothetical and may be difficult to answer. But try to imagine wanting the event as much as you did, but not hoping for it. Compared to simply wanting or desiring the event, in what ways do you think you acted differently *because of your hope*?

For each description, subjects could mark "not at all" (0), "somewhat" (1), or "very much" (2). The results are shown in Table 1.4.

What people do in a situation is obviously influenced by what they believe they can do. Therefore, in Table 1.4, results are reported separately for subjects who believed they

---

[1] The results presented in Table 1.3 are worth emphasizing for methodological as well as for theoretical reasons. Retrospective self-reports of affective experience are especially prone to bias and distortion. Yet, subjects did not simply report feelings that, according to the cultural stereotype, should accompany hope. True, they did report feeling better and more confident after beginning to hope, but on the whole (i.e., in terms of main effects) they did not report being less anxious, helpless, depressed, and so forth. For the most part, subjects were sensitive to the circumstances surrounding the particular episodes in question.

Table 1.4.   Mean ratings of instrumental responses attributed to hope, and differences between groups[a] of subjects who perceived events to be primarily under personal or situational control.

		Differences between groups			
Action taken	Total sample (n=150)	Personal control (n=61)	Situational control (n=57)	t	p
I worked harder; was more persistent in my efforts	1.19	1.41	.95	-3.27	<.01
I became better organized; got my act together	.96	1.11	.73	-2.84	<.01
I thought about the issue in a more imaginative and creative way	.87	.91	.80	-.87	ns
I took added risks; stuck my neck out	.63	.67	.45	-1.83	<.10
I relaxed my efforts; relied on faith	.62	.55	.78	1.76	<.10
I became cautious, played it safe	.57	.64	.56	-.64	ns
I put the issue out of my mind; started to concentrate on other things	.29	.30	.30	.03	ns
Other[b]					

Note. Each item was rated on a scale from 0 = not at all, 1 = somewhat, 2 = very much.

[a]In forming these groups, the 32 subjects who marked the midpoint ("5") of the control scale were excluded.

[b]Eleven subjects (7.3%) marked "other." Their statements were generally emphatic restatements of one of the descriptions provided.

had greater or lesser control over the outcome. These two groups were formed as follows. As will be recalled from an earlier analysis (the objects of hope), subjects rated their perceived control over the event on an 11-point scale. The scale ran from 0 ("completely due to factors under your own control") to 10 ("completely due to factors beyond your control"). Thus, lower numbers represent greater personal-control, whereas higher numbers represent greater situational control. The personal-control group listed in Table 1.4 (n=61) consists of subjects with ratings of 4 or below; and the situational-control group (n=57) consists of subjects with ratings of 6 or above. Subjects who rated the midpoint of the scale (n=32) were dropped from these analyses.

The most frequently reported response among both groups of subjects was to "work harder." Specifically, 88.5% of the subjects in the personal-control group reported working "somewhat" or "very much" harder because of their hope; 63.2% of the subjects in the situational- control group did so. Other common responses were "to become better organized" and "to think about the issue in a more imaginative and creative way." These results attest to the strength of the link between hope and action, especially when some response is possible.

Terminating Conditions

As with the question regarding eliciting circumstances discussed earlier (see Table 1.2), subjects were asked to indicate the reasons they stopped hoping. A variety of possible reasons were offered, and subjects were asked to check the *one* that best described their episodes. Again, open-ended responses to pilot questionnaires provided the basis for the descriptions. The frequencies of the various responses are shown in Table 1.5.

In roughly 50% of the episodes, hope was terminated because the person obtained what he or she was hoping for. However, hopes also were terminated due to changes in the person's evaluation of the situation. Reductions in the perceived probability or importance of the event, as well as

Table 1.5. Change in circumstance that terminated episodes of hope.

Change in circumstance	Percentage of subjects endorsing item
I obtained what I was hoping for.	52.3%
I decided there was little chance of obtaining what I was hoping for (although it was still possible).	16.1%
The time passed when the event I was hoping for could have occurred, and it didn't.	6.7%
I came to realize that what I was hoping for was completely under my own control; that is, I could make it happen.	6.7%
I no longer wanted what I had been hoping for.	2.7%
Other[a]	15.4%

[a]8 of the 23 subjects who marked "other" (5% of the total sample) described situations in which their hope suddenly became impossible (e.g., "received a rejection letter from the school I was hoping to attend"). The remainder of the "other" responses involved variations of one or more of the descriptions provided.

increases in perceived control, all served to terminate episodes (see Table 1.5).

Fulfilled vs Unfilled Hope

When subjects whose hopes were fulfilled (roughly 50% of the total, as indicated in Table 1.5) were contrasted with the remaining subjects whose hopes were unfulfilled for one reason or another, a number of significant differences emerged. For example, fulfilled hopes were evaluated more positively than were unfulfilled hopes. Also, subjects whose hopes were fulfilled rated the object of their hope as more important and saw their chances of success as greater. To an unknown extent, these results may reflect actual differences in the events hoped for. That is, the more probable an event, the more likely it is to occur; and the more important an event, the more a person may work for its fulfillment. However, possible distortions due to hindsight should not be overlooked. People tend to overestimate the prior probabilities of events that have actually occurred (a phenomenon called "creeping determinism" by Fischoff, 1975). Similarly, cognitive dissonance could influence the judged value or importance of fulfilled versus unfulfilled hopes.

In order to guard against retrospective distortions, separate analyses were performed on all variables for the groups reporting fulfilled and unfulfilled hopes. The results of these analyses require no qualifications of the findings presented thus far. However, they are relevant to the findings reported next.

Retrospective Evaluations

When people meet their own and society's expectations, they usually feel good and self-satisfied. When their behavior falls short of expectations, they tend to feel bad and dissatisfied. Knowledge of the conditions that lead to either dissatisfaction or satisfaction can thus provide insights into the rules that help constitute and regulate behavior.

In the present study, subjects were asked to make retrospective evaluations of their hope by responding to a list of seven adjectives that described possible feelings and attitudes about the episode. The adjectives were: indifferent, amused, embarrassed, ambivalent, proud, satisfied with yourself, and dissatisfied with yourself. Subjects indicated the extent to which each adjective reflected their feelings about the episode by marking "not at all" (0), "somewhat" (1), or "very much" (2).

Correlations among the adjectives, as well as logical considerations, indicated that four could be combined into a single dimension, anchored on the positive end by "proud" and "satisfied with yourself" and on the negative end by "embarrassed" and "dissatisfied with yourself." Scores on this new "embarrassed-proud" dimension were obtained by subtracting the sum of the two negative ratings from the sum of the two positive ratings, and hence could range from "-4" to "+4," with a midpoint of "0." The actual mean for all subjects was a positive 1.60 (S.D.=1.95).

In order to assess which characteristics of hope were associated with positive self-feelings, correlations were computed between the embarrassed-proud dimension, on the one hand, and appraisals of the objects of hope and the various actions taken because of hope, on the other. Table 1.6 presents those variables that showed statistically significant correlations for all subjects taken together (p <.05, two-tailed). Correlations were also computed for various subgroups, namely, those subjects whose hopes were fulfilled versus those whose hopes were not, and those who believed they could exert control over events versus those who believed events were under situational control.

The rationale for forming the subgroups presented in Table 1.6 was as follows. Subjects whose hopes were fulfilled reported being more proud and self-satisfied (mean rating = 2.55) than did subjects whose hopes were unfulfilled (mean rating = .55; p <.001). Since retrospective evaluations are sensitive to distortion as a function of the outcome of an episode, the correlations are presented in Table 6 for the fulfilled and unfulfilled groups separately. Correlations that are significant within each group, as well as for the entire sample, can be considered particularly reliable.

Similar considerations apply to the variable of perceived control. With regard to instrumental responses, especially, subjects who believed they had some control over the outcome responded differently than did those who believed the outcome was situationally determined (see Table 1.4). Therefore, correlations are also presented separately in Table 1.6 for groups reporting personal and situational control. (In forming these groups, it may be recalled, the 32 subjects who

Table 1.6. Correlations of retrospective evaluations ("embarrassed-proud" dimension) with ratings of the appraised object of hope and actions taken because of hope. Correlations are presented separately for the total sample, and for subgroups based on the outcome of the episode (fulfilled versus unfulfilled) and perceived control over the outcome (personal versus situational control).

	All Subjects (n=150)	Subgroups			
		Fulfilled (n=78)	Unfulfilled (n=72)	Personal Control (n=61)	Situational Control (n=57)
Appraised object					
average probability	.28**	.12	.16	.27*	.22
average importance	.27**	.18	.19	.34**	.33*
Actions taken because of hope					
worked harder	.31**	.22*	.29*	.48**	.25
became better organized	.23**	.20	.27**	.30*	.10
became cautious	-.17*	.08	-.38**	-.30*	.09

*p <.05, two tailed

**p <.01, two tailed

marked the midpoint of the control scale were eliminated. It should also be noted that there was no interaction between perceived control and the outcome of an episode—56% of the personal-control group and 58% of the situational-control group reported that their hopes were fulfilled.)

In considering the results presented in Table 1.6, let us begin with the correlations between the embarrassed-proud dimension and the appraised object. The correlations with probability of attainment were significant for the entire sample, and for the personal- and situational-control groups separately. The correlations within the fulfilled and unfulfilled groups were in the expected direction, but they were not statistically significant. For the most part, then, these results are consistent with the notion that hopes *should* be realistic.

Similar relations were obtained with respect to the perceived importance of the objects. That is, subjects tended to report being proud and self-satisfied when the objects of their hope were regarded as important.

Among the actions subjects believed they took because of their hope, the one that correlated most highly with subsequent pride and self-satisfaction was "worked harder." This relation was stable across all groups; even subjects who saw the outcome of an episode to be largely out of their control apparently felt more satisfied if they took some action. "Became better organized" also showed positive and relatively consistent correlations with subsequent evaluations. On the other hand, subjects who reported that they "became cautious" because of their hope tended to be less proud and self-satisfied afterwards; at least this was true of those subjects who also believed they had some control over the outcome and/or who reported that their hopes went unfulfilled.

In short, the data reported in Table 1.6 suggest three general principles. Specifically, people should limit their hope to things (a) that have a reasonable chance of attainment and (b) that are important; also (c) people should be ready to act to achieve their hoped-for goals, if there is any opportunity to do so. To the extent that these principles are violated, people tend to feel embarrassed and dissatisfied with themselves (or, at least, less proud and self-satisfied).

It may be noted that the first two of these principles (realism and importance) were also identified in an earlier section comparing hope with want and desire. A third principle identified in that earlier section had to do with moral values—person should not hope for things that are personally or socially unacceptable. The fact that this third principle did not appear in the present data is easily explained. In selecting representative episodes, subjects tended not to choose instances of hope that violated the principle. The present data on representative episodes do, however, make explicit a principle only hinted at earlier, namely, hope calls for action, if action is possible. This makes four general principles in all, about which we will have more to say shortly.

Forbidden Hopes

The reports of representative episodes of hope provide a good picture of the times in which hope is appropriate. We now explore the rules of hope from another direction, namely, by considering the conditions under which hope is *inappropriate*.

Toward the end of the questionnaire subjects were asked to describe an event that might make their lives easier and more enjoyable, but that they believed they should not hope for. On the basis of open- ended responses to pilot questionnaires, a list of possible reasons why a person should not hope for an event was provided, and subjects were asked to check each item that applied. The results are presented in Table 1.7.

The item endorsed most often involves the probability of the event. In over a third of the cases, subjects indicated that hope would be inappropriate because the chances of attainment were too low. This supports the idea that hope is appropriate primarily in situations that have a reasonable chance of fulfillment.

Three other items (up to fate, only hard work will achieve it, and easily achieved) address the connection between hope and action. Hope is not appropriate when personal effort is either entirely futile or else certain to yield the desired effect.

Subjects also indicated that they would not hope for things that "would interfere with other goals or involve too much work or responsibility." The implication here is that hope should take priority; if an otherwise desirable event requires the sacrifice of a more highly valued goal, then it is an inappropriate object of hope.

Finally, social acceptability excluded many events (e.g., those regarded as "materialistic," "selfish," or "immoral") from being appropriate objects of hope. The link between hope and virtue, so prominent in classical theological doctrine, is also apparent in our everyday conception of hope.

Table 1.7. Reasons for not hoping for something that might make life easier or more enjoyable.

Reasons	Percentage of subjects endorsing item[a]
The event is unrealistic (can't happen); hope would be an illusion.	35.3%
The event will or will not occur, regardless of your efforts (it is up to fate); hope will not make any difference.	29.3%
The event is impractical or disadvantageous at the present time (e.g., because it would interfere with other goals, or involve too much work or responsibility); it would be unwise to hope for it.	28.7%
Only hard work will achieve the event; hope itself would not help.	28.0%
The event is socially unacceptable or inappropriate (e.g., because it is too materialistic, selfish, or immoral); it would not be right to hope for it.	16.7%
The event is easily achieved; there is no need to hope.	4.7%
The event is trivial or unimportant; it is not worth hoping for.	4.7%
Other (please specify)[b]	21.3%

[a]Subjects could endorse as many items as they deemed applicable; hence, the percentages add to more than 100%.

[b]The reasons listed under the "other" category were generally variations on one or more of the listed themes.

Discussion: Prototypic Rules of Hope

Data have now been presented from three different sources: a comparison of hope to want and desire, detailed analyses of representative episodes of hope, and reports of forbidden hopes. All three sources yield converging evidence for four overarching rules of hope. We will call these prudential rules, moralistic rules, priority rules, and action rules.

Prudential rules. One of the most consistent findings to emerge from the data thus far is an emphasis on realism. By definition, almost, hope involves future uncertainties; but the uncertainties should not be too great. When the probability of attainment is unrealistically low, hope is inappropriate. Or, stated more positively, hope should be prudent; it is, in the words of Lynch (1965), "realistic imagination."

Moralistic rules. The object of hope is circumscribed not only by what is prudent or reasonable, but also by what is personally and socially acceptable, i.e., by moral values. This aspect of hope becomes most apparent when hope is compared with simple wants and desires. A person might desire an event (e.g., the death of a rich relative) for which he would not hope. Hope is related to a person's system of values in a way that wants, desires and fantasies are not.

Priority rules. By "priority" we mean that hope takes precedence over other wants or desires. The object of hope should touch upon a person's vital interests; in fact, if the object of hope is of sufficient importance, prudential and moralistic rules may be set aside. This is not to say that people do not sometimes hope for trivial events. They often do. That, however, is the exception and not the rule.[2]

---

[2]   The tendency of subjects to rate the objects of hope as important is also evident from two pilot studies. In one of these studies, subjects were asked to choose a representative episode of hope from the previous *week* (as opposed to the previous year, as in the present study, but without stipulation with regard to beginning or ending). The mean ratings of importance for these episodes was 7.8, which was not significantly different from the 8.2 rating obtained in the main study reported here. In another pilot study, one group of subjects was asked to describe an *intense* episode of hope which had begun and ended during the previous year, and another

Action rules. People who hope should be willing to take appropriate action to achieve their goals, if action is possible. Action rules are evident in the present data in a variety of ways. For example, with the exception of altruistic hopes (which concern the fate of another person), there was a tendency for subjects to hope for things that were partially--but not totally--under personal control. Also, subjects reported working harder because of their hope, even when they believed they had little control over events. And when they were not working harder, they reported thinking about the issue in a more creative way. Even "relying on faith," frequently reported by subjects with little perceived control, is an active response, at least in comparison to "putting the issue out of mind," which was seldom endorsed by any of the subjects.

The above rules are stated in very general terms. They might better be conceived of as "rule prototypes" rather than as rules per se. That is, they are more like guiding principles (e.g., "Drive safely") than they are like specific regulations (e.g., "Don't exceed 55 miles per hour"). What constitutes safe driving may vary considerably, depending on the capabilities of the driver and the conditions of the road. Similarly, the rules of hope may be instantiated differently, depending on the capabilities of the individual and the surrounding circumstances.[3]

Needless to say, the rules of hope are frequently violated, although in many instances the violations may be more apparent than real. As was mentioned earlier, apparent

---

group described a *mild* episode. The ratings of importance were 7.8 and 7.6 for the intense and mild episodes, respectively. Again, the differences were not statistically significant. It appears, then, that hoped for events are regularly evaluated at approximately the same level of importance whether the episode is drawn from the past week or the past year, and whether it is mild or intense. Indeed, the very notion of a "mild hope" seems almost self-contradictory. A hope may have only a slight chance of fulfillment, but modifiers such as "slight," "mild," "little," and the like, do not seem to apply to hope per se, except perhaps in a pejorative sense (e.g., "Little people hope for little things").

violations may be largely the result of the difference between subjective and objective appraisals of the situation.   For example, many people hope for world peace or to win a lottery.   In both cases the objective likelihood of the event is well below the range of probabilities indicated by prudential rules; and personal control is low, which makes the application action rules difficult.   Nevertheless, at a "gut level" the relevant probabilities may be assessed much more positively, and persons may act as though they had greater control than they actually do.   Hope is, after all, an emotion, and emotional judgments typically involve "magical thinking," the creation of a surreality (Sartre, 1948; Solomon, 1976).

The rules of hope will be considered again in Studies 3 and 4 when we examine metaphors of hope and compare American and Korean hopes.   But first, in the next chapter, we explore what it means to say that hope is an emotion.

---

[3] When stated in broad, prototypic form, prudential rules, moralistic rules, priority rules, and action rules are not unique to hope, but can apply to other emotions as well.   Anger, for example, should also be prudent, moral, about important issues, and action oriented (Averill, 1982).

II

Study 2:
An Emotion of the Mind

A major purpose of this series of studies was to investigate the nature of emotions, using hope as a paradigm case. While Study 1 identified a set of rules that define hope as a coherent syndrome, those rules say little in regards to whether or not hope is, in fact, an emotion. In the present study, we address that question through a comparison of hope to other, more prototypic emotions, namely, anger and love.

Because the emotions do not form a discrete, clearly defined category, one of the major goals of this study was to identify the criteria by which we decide whether a particular syndrome is, or is not, an emotion. For the sake of clarity, we will call the similarities that help unite the category of emotions, *parameters*, to distinguish them from the *rules* that help constitute particular syndromes. The distinction between parameters and rules is somewhat arbitrary, but nevertheless useful. Parameters set the stage, so to speak, and rules dictate the lines. Together, they help define a *model* of behavior, in this case, an emotional model.

We will have much more to say about models of behavior in Chapter 5, after we have presented the data from the entire series of studies. For the moment, suffice it to say that acts that are understood to fall within an emotional model are both experienced by the individual and judged by others very differently from acts that fall within, say, a rational or purposive model of behavior. The starkest example of this distinction is in courts of law. A homicide might be adjudicated as a crime of passion, which presumes an emotional model, or as murder, which presumes a rational/purposive model ("malice aforethought"). (A third possibility exists, namely, the homicide might be attributed to insanity, which presumes a medical model.) It is important to note that precisely the same behavior may be involved in each cas— what differs is how the behavior is interpreted.

Though relatively few acts are ever formally interpreted in a court of law, virtually all acts are interpreted at the moment of occurrence by observers and actors alike. When an emotional model is perceived to apply (usually implicitly and without any conscious deliberation), a special set of behaviors—including internal states—are deemed appropriate. Because of this, the question of hope's status as an emotion (i.e., the applicability of an emotional model to hope) has considerable bearing on the actual experience and expression of hope.

Models of emotion may be either formal, as in psychological theory, or informal, as in the "implicit theory" of the proverbial person in the street. As we discussed in the Introduction to this book, contemporary psychological theory has tended to exclude hope from the category of emotion. From a social-constructionist point of view, however, a more important issue is whether or not hope conforms to the popular conception (folk model) of emotion, and if so, what the parameters of that model are.

Method

Methodologically, Study 2 was a continuation of Study 1; that is, the same subjects and procedures were used in both studies. More specifically, the last part of the questionnaire used in Study 1 (see Appendix) posed the following "thought experiment" for subjects:

Think for a moment about two commonly recognized emotions, such as anger and love. What do they have in common, such that they are both classified as emotions? Now compare hope with anger and love (not separately, but in terms of their common features).

Subjects were instructed to list in spaces provided "two ways in which hope is similar to anger and love" and "two ways in which hope is different from anger and love." This was the first time in the questionnaire that hope was linked in any way with emotional states.

Results

The above procedure yielded 287 similarities (13 of the 150 subjects could think of only one way in which hope was similar to anger and love) and 289 differences (11 subjects could think of only 1 difference). The responses were analyzed in the same manner as those distinguishing hope from want, as described in Study 1. The results of these content-analyses are presented in Table 2.1.

The similarities between hope, anger, and love are listed in the left-hand column of Table 2.1, and the differences in the right-hand column. To facilitate comparison, similarities have been aligned with differences whenever there is some correspondence in the underlying dimensions. Additionally, the categories have been grouped into subsections, depending upon whether they deal primarily with the subjective aspects of the experience, the object of the emotion, behavior, and consequences. Within each subsection, the categories have

Table 2.1. Similarities (n = 287) and differences (n = 289) between hope, anger, and love.

Similarities	Differences
	General Classification	

All are emotions (8.4%)   Hope is not an emotion (3.5%)
All are feelings (7.7%)

With respect to subjective experience

All are difficult to   Hope is easier to control (4.2%)
control (6.3%)   Hope is more difficult to control (2.1%)

All affect the way you think   Hope is less real; it is like
about or perceive events, e.g.,   a dream, fantasy, or illusion
in obsessional, irrational,   (4.5%)
or illusory ways (5.6%)

All can be intense   Hope is less intense or strong
experiences (2.8%)   (2.4%)

All can be accompanied   Hope is more consistently
by pleasant and/or   pleasant, or involves less pain,
unpleasant experiences   at least while it is occurring
(2.8%)   (2.8%)

All are highly personal   Hope is more self-initiated, i.e.,
experiences; they come   it is more dependent on internal
from the "inside" (2.1%)   than external conditions (3.1%)

All are indescribable,   Hope is more difficult to
intangible, and/or   describe; it is diffuse,
abstract experiences (1.7%)   intangible (2.1%)

                                  Hope is more cognitive, e.g.,
                                  a state of mind, attitude,
                                  thought process (2.1%)

                                  Hope is more like a want, desire
                                  or wish (2.1%)

Table 2.1 continued

Similarities	*Differences*
	With respect to the object
All are directed toward external things or events (2.1%)	A person can hope for a greater variety of things; hope is not limited to specific people and their actions (4.5%)
	The object of hope is more uncertain, doubtful, less realistic (3.1%)
	Hope is more often associated with future events (3.1%)
	With respect to behavior
All affect the way you behave, e.g., leading you to act in different or unusual ways (4.9%)	Hope is less demonstrable; it is not so easily expressed (9.4%)
All motivate behavior, increase persistence, enable one to keep going (4.9%)	Hope is more characteristically motivating; it sustains, and gives direction to behavior (1.7%)
All can be--and often are-- expressed outwardly, e.g., in gestures, words, or actions (2.1%)	
All are states of high arousal or energy levels (1.7%)	
	With respect to consequences
All can have cathartic effect, provide a release of tension or a sense of satisfaction (2.3%)	Hope is more constructive; it more often leads to positive outcomes (2.4%)

Table 2.1 continued

Similarities	*Differences*
	Miscellaneous	

<u>All are common or universal experiences</u> (3.8%)	A person is seldom without hope (1.7%)
All are a necessary part of life (2.1%)	
All can come or go quickly, are subject to sudden change (1.7%)	Hope is more clearly demarcated temporally; it can come to an abrupt end (when achieved or nor achieved), be forgotten, or change focus (3.1%)
	<u>Hope is more of an individual or private matter; it need not involve other people</u> (4.2%)

Note.--The five most frequently mentioned categories in both columns are underlined (excluding the classification of all three states--hope, anger and love--as emotions and/or feelings among the similarities).   At least five responses (1.7%) were required to form a category; 37% of the similarities and 38% of the differences were either too idiosyncratic or too vague to be categorized.

been ordered from the most to the least frequently mentioned similarities. (To form a category, at least 5 exemplars were required—representing 1.7% of the total number of responses).

One final point by way of introduction: The percentages listed in Table 2.1 give a good indication of the relative importance of various features, but they are misleadingly low in an absolute sense.   This is for three reasons. First, they are based on the spontaneous responses of subjects. The failure to mention a feature does not necessarily imply disagreement. Second, responses were classified according to the dominant theme, and many responses could have been placed in more than one category. For example, one subject responded, "All three are intensely emotional feelings." This response could have been placed in the "intense experience" category, the "emotion" category, or the "feeling" category. It was placed in the last, because that seemed to be the major emphasis of the response.   Third, each subject gave two responses; thus, in most instances the percentage of subjects mentioning an item is roughly double the percentage of responses listed in Table 2.1.

Similarities

Consider first the left-hand column of Table 2.1. The most frequently mentioned similarities were that all three states–hope, anger, and love–are emotions (8.4% of the responses) or feelings (7.7%). For the reasons stated above, these percentages considerably underestimate the amount of agreement with respect to these two categories. If secondary and not just dominant responses were counted, and if the results were expressed as the percentage of subjects rather than of responses, then approximately half the subjects explicitly mentioned that hope, like anger and love, is an emotion and/or a feeling.[1]

---

[1] We emphasize this fact because of the tendency among contemporary theorists to ignore hope as a *real* emotion. Several other studies relevant to this issue are also worth noting briefly. In one study (Averill, 1975, Berkeley sample), subjects rated 535 emotional terms on a 7-point scale. A rating of "1" meant that practically nobody, in the subject's opinion, would consider that the term referred to an emotion; a rating of "7" indicated that most everybody would agree that it referred to an emotion. The term "hopeful" received a rating of 5.42, placing it at the 72nd percentile of the 535 terms, ahead of such terms as proud (5.08), amazed (4.99), guilty (4.91), contemptuous (4.88), and amused (4.74). Similar results have been reported by Shaver, Schwartz, Karson, & O'Conner (1987). In another study (Fehr & Russell, 1984, Study 1), 200 subjects were asked to list as many instances of the category "emotion" as came readily to mind. Eight subjects mentioned "hope." This is not a large number, but it placed hope at the 70th percentile of the frequency distribution of those emotions mentioned more than once (196 emotions in all). Hope was mentioned more frequently than such states as cheerful (7 times), shyness (6), panic (5), shame (4), wonder (3), and contempt (2). In short, hope is not as prototypic an emotion as either anger or love, yet hope is more representative of emotion than are some states (e.g., disgust, contempt, interest) that are frequently posited as fundamental emotions by contemporary theorists (see, for example, Izard, 1977; Ekman, 1984).

The remaining similarities listed in Table 2.1 represent characteristics that hope shares in common with other emotions. The five most frequently mentioned characteristics (underlined) are that hope, like anger and love, is difficult to control (6.3% of the responses), affects the way you think (5.6%) or behave (4.9%), motivates behavior (4.9%), and is a common or universal experiences (3.8%). If one wished to construct a paradigm of emotion as conceived of in this culture, these and the remaining similarities listed in Table 2.1 would provide a good starting point.

Differences

Now let us consider the ways that hope differs from other emotions (the right-hand column of Table 2.1). Some subjects (3.5% of the total responses, or about 7% of the subjects) indicated that they did not consider hope to be an emotion at all. But that was clearly a minority opinion.

The most frequently mentioned difference (9.4% of the responses) was with respect to behavior; specifically, hope is less demonstrable than anger or love. There are characteristic ways of expressing these latter emotions, but hope although it is action oriented—need not be expressed in any particular way.

The next two most frequently mentioned differences had to do with the experience and the object of hope, respectively. Experientially, hope is considered less real; or, stated affirmatively, hope is more like a dream, fantasy, or illusion (4.5% of the responses).[2] With regard to the object of hope, people are relatively unrestricted in what they can hope for (also 4.5% of the responses). Anger and love are tied to particular events or targets, e.g., an unwarranted affront in the case of anger or a certain individual in the case of love. By contrast, a person can hope for almost anything, within the bounds set by the rules of hope, as discussed previously.

---

[2] When interpreting this difference, one should keep in mind the results presented in the previous section, on the contrast between hope and fantasy (see Table 1.7, especially).

There is no need to comment on the other differences listed in Table 2.1. For the most part, they are self-explanatory.

Which are more important from a theoretical perspective: The features that hope shares with other emotions or the ways in which it differs? Most recent theories have emphasized the differences, even to the extent of excluding hope from the domain of the emotional. We will use the similarities as a starting point for our own analysis.

Discussion: Hope as an Emotion

To recapitulate briefly, the five most frequently mentioned similarities between hope, anger, and love (other than that all are emotions/feelings) were that (a) all are difficult to control; (b) they affect the way you think; (c) they lead you to act in uncharacteristic ways; (d) they motivate behavior; and (e) they are common or universal experiences. These similarities represent the main parameters of our folk model or implicit theory of hope as an emotion. Let us consider each in turn.

(a) Hope, like anger and love, is difficult to control. A central feature of our folk model is the idea that people have little control over their emotional responses. Stated in somewhat antiquated terminology, emotions belong to the category of passivity (Aristotle, 1941 edition). More colloquially, we "fall" in love, are "overcome" by anger, "can't help" but hope, and so forth. The idea that people lack control over their emotions has been called by Solomon (1976) the "myth of the passions." People may in fact have much more control over their emotions than they realize. However, it is not so much the experience of passivity that is a myth as the explanations that have often been offered for the experience. In contemporary psychology it is common to attribute the passionate quality of emotions to "instincts," that is, to automatic reactions that have been "hard wired" into our nervous system during the course of biological evolution. The essential idea is that, given an adequate stimulus or set of

circumstances, certain behaviors automatically occur. Hope does fit this idea, for it is not associated with any specific physiological responses or reflex-like reactions.

How, then, can we account for the apparent passivity that hope shares with other emotions? A complete answer to this question will have to wait until we have presented the results of Studies 3 and 4 in subsequent chapters. However, a few preliminary observations can be made at this point. To begin, let us distinguish between two phases of an emotion: The first is an assessment of the situation; and the second is the behavioral response (including physiological changes) to that assessment.[3] Most contemporary theories associate the experience of passivity—of lack of control—with the response phase. However, passivity can just as well be associated with the assessment phase. Indeed, the paradigm case of an action—as opposed to a passion—is not a behavioral response, but a rational judgment. By way of antithesis, nonrational judgments historically have been classified as passions. This was the view of ancient Stoics, who equated the emotions with false judgments; it is also the view of such contemporary theorists as Solomon (1976), who view emotions as evaluative judgments.

To say that a judgment is nonrational does not imply that it is either imprudent or without good reason. It implies, rather, that the norms of rationality (e.g., as exemplified by rules of logic) are not necessarily relevant in the situation. The "reasonableness" of an emotional judgment is to be evaluated primarily by the extent to which it conforms with the prevailing rules both of emotion generally and the particular emotion specifically. Anger, too, has its rules (Averill, 1982), as does love (Averill, 1985).

When confronted with a situation in which the rules of hope apply, an individual usually "can't help" but hope.

---

[3] It must be emphasized that the distinction between the assessment phase and the response phase of an emotional episode is primarily analytical—like distinguishing between the concave and convex sides of an arc. In actuality, the assessment phase is part of the emotion, a kind of response in its own right, and not an antecedent condition external to the emotion.

In this regard, hope is every bit as passive as any of the more prototypic emotions. The difference beween hope and other emotions lies primarily in the fact that once an appropriate assessment or appraisal has been made, no specific behavioral response is dictated. As will be discussed below, hope does affect the ways one thinks and acts, but these responses are not seen to be so directly and uniquely associated with hope as are the responses associated with anger and love.

(b) *Hope affects the way you think and (c) it leads you to act in uncharacteristic ways.* These two similarities between hope, anger, and love can best be considered together, for their implications are similar. It order to highlight those implications, let us also note one of the major *differences* between hope and other emotions. Specifically, hope is more like a state of mind—an attitude, dream, fantasy, and so forth. In a word, hope is more *cognitive* than most other emotions. This feature, perhaps more than any other, has led some theorists to exclude hope from the category of emotions. Therefore, the ways that an emotion may and may not be "cognitive" deserves careful consideration.

The notion of cognition is poorly defined in psychology. For many psychologists, "cognition" refers to all activities that are not interpreted in a strictly physiological or behavioral way. In this broad sense, "cognitive" has simply replaced the older concept of "mental," the latter having fallen into disrepute during the heyday of behaviorism. Nothing precludes emotions from being cognitive in this extended sense. Hope, at least, can hardly be interpreted otherwise.

In the vernacular, "cognition" is used in a more restricted sense, namely, to refer to the "intellectual processes by which knowledge is gained" (*Webster's Third New International Dictionary*). Cognition is also frequently used by psychologists in this restricted sense (cf. Chomsky, 1980). One implication of this narrow conception is that emotions are noncognitive.

Now let us return to the two similarities under consideration, namely, that hope, anger, and love all "affect the way you think about or perceive events, e.g., in obsessional, irrational, or illusory ways"; and all affect "the way you behave, e.g., leading you to act in different or unusual ways."

These features are hardly indicative of the kinds of processes "by which knowledge is gained."

The fact that hope may lead a person to think and act in nonrational—even irrational—ways might at first seem inconsistent with prudential rules, which stipulate that hope should be realistic (i.e., there should be a reasonable chance of fulfillment). However, as we have pointed out, when something is sufficiently important, people may convince themselves that chances are better than they actually are. That assessment is not rational, nor are numerous thoughts, feelings and actions that may be part of the ensuing episode of hope. (Of course, similar observations could be made with regard to love, which should be realistic but not necessarily rational. Even anger, a more negatively viewed emotion, is not generally without its reasons—cf. Averill, 1982.)

To summarize, hope differs from other emotions in being a largely "cognitive" state, broadly defined. But this does not preclude hope from conforming to an emotional model in which "cognition" is defined more narrowly to mean essentially "rational." In the latter sense, hope is noncognitive (nonrational).

(d) Hope motivates behavior. Traditional psychological theories, as well as our folk model, have often treated emotions as concomitants of, or varieties of, motives (Arnold, 1960; Buck, 1985; Frijda, 1986). Hope, too, can be conceived of in this way. Thus, according to Bloch (1959/1986), hope is experienced as an emotion because it stems from deeply seated motives or drives which, when consciously experienced, are felt as impulses to action. This is in essential agreement with the action rules of hope identified in Study 1.

A major source of debate among emotion theorists concerns the origins of the motive or impulse to a action. As discussed above, most contemporary theorists maintain that, at least for the basic emotions, the motives must be innate or "instinctive." That is not Bloch's position—nor ours—with respect to hope. No *specific* feelings or responses are associated with hope, contrary to what would be implied by the notion that hope is a biologically based, instinctive reaction. But open-endedness should not disqualify hope from the category of emotion—even those emotions considered basic.

Deep seated drives may be socially induced or even idiosyncratic to the individual.

(e) *Hope is a universal experience.* This brings us to the last of the five most frequently mentioned similarities between hope, anger, and love: All are believed to be universal. This fact, if true, might be taken as support for the notion that hope is indeed a biologically based, species-wide phenomenon. But to what extent is hope universal? We tend to believe that what is vital to our own lives must also be vital to the lives of others. However, as we shall see in Chapter 4, where American and Korean conceptions of hope are compared, hope *as an emotion* is not necessarily universal.

To conclude, there are ample grounds for classifying hope among the emotions, at least the way hope is conceived of in our own culture. Hope conforms to the major parameters of the emotional model, namely, it is difficult to control (and is thus a passion rather than an action), it is noncognitive (in the narrow sense, but not in the broad sense), and it motivates behavior. The major difference between hope and (some) other emotions is that hope is less demonstrable. That is, there are no expressive reactions or instrumental responses specific to hope. We would contend, however, that contemporary theories of emotion have been unduly biased by an overemphasis on response mechanisms. This is an issue to which we will return in Chapter 5, following a presentation of Studies 3 and 4.

III

Study 3:
Metaphors and Maxims

The use of questionnaires, as in Studies 1 and 2, is one way of investigating the way people think about emotions. Another way is through an examination of the language that people use to communicate their thoughts and feelings. It is largely through language that we conceive, construct, and legitimize our everyday social reality (Berger & Luckmann, 1966). In this chapter we examine the implicit theories of hope as reflected in maxims, folk sayings, and colloquialisms. More explicitly, we examine the metaphors found in these figures of speech. Kovecses (1986, 1988; Lakoff & Kovecses, 1983) has used metaphors to reconstruct the cognitive models of anger and love implicit among Americans. We follow his example in broad outline.

Characteristics of Metaphors

Metaphors enrich our understanding by linking phenomena from two different domains of discourse. One domain serves as the *source* and the other as the *target* of the metaphor. For example, in the metaphorical expression, "the machinery of the mind," the source is "machinery" and the target is "the mind." The metaphor implies that knowledge about the workings of machines can, in some (unspecified) sense, be extended to an understanding of mental activity.

Metaphors can be distinguished along a variety of dimensions. One of the most important of these distinctions is that between *basic-level* and *abstract* metaphors (Lakoff & Kovecses, 1983). Basic-level metaphors are, for the most part, the actual metaphors used in common speech. They are rich in imagery and closely linked to everyday experience. They allow us to draw inferences from the source to the target domain, using our knowledge of the familiar. Abstract metaphors, by contrast, represent superordinate categories. They provide the implicit rationale for the basic-level metaphors. To illustrate, the abstract metaphor of emotion as force or energy provides the rationale for many basic-level metaphors, of which the following are a few examples: "He was driven by fear"; "She was bursting with pride"; "He couldn't contain his anger"; and "Love makes the world go 'round." (See Averill, in press b, for a historical review of this and other abstract metaphors of emotion.)

Another important distinction is between *literary* and *explanatory* metaphors (Gentner & Grudin, 1985). A literary metaphor is like a stage setting: it conveys a general orientation, attitude, or mood from the source to the target domain. An explanatory metaphor, which is more common in scientific discourse, is designed to convey specific information. Explanatory metaphors require that the structure and function of objects in the source domain correspond closely with the structure and function of objects in the target domain, so that knowledge about the source can be applied to the target.

A distinction can also be made between *idiosyncratic* and *conventional* metaphors. Idiosyncratic metaphors are novel and original; they can often be attributed to a single person (although they may be quoted often by others). Such metaphors are common in maxims and folk sayings. Conventional metaphors are stylized, abbreviated sayings, as in many colloquialisms. An example of idiosyncratic metaphor would be Emily Dickenson's characterization of hope as "the thing with feathers that perches in the soul." The expression, "a ray of hope," is highly conventionalized.

Finally, metaphors may be more or less *productive* in any of three ways: (a) the number of lexical variations on a common theme; (b) the frequency of use; and (c) the amount of information transferred from the source to the target domain. Each of these ways will be illustrated shortly.

Methods

Metaphorical expressions were collected from books of maxims and folk sayings, thesauri, and dictionaries. In addition, 59 subjects (undergraduate students participating in another research project) were asked to list three slang expressions related to hope, and these expressions were screened for metaphors. Finally, a few metaphors were obtained from miscellaneous sources (political speeches, novels, and the like).

An initial screening of the above sources yielded a list of roughly 300 potential metaphors. The criteria for inclusion in this initial list were open-ended; the goal was to be inclusive rather than exclusive. To refine the list, the potential metaphors were assessed by three judges. Expressions were eliminated if they were judged too idiosyncratic, too general (i.e., applicable to a wide variety of states other than hope), or too vague. Disagreements among the judges were resolved through discussion.

To reduce the list further, near redundancies were eliminated. That is, if different metaphorical expressions employed the same basic terms, only one instance was retained. For example, there are many variations on the theme, originally adumbrated by Aristotle, that hope is a dream of a person who is awake. These were all consolidated into one "dream" metaphor. Also, for consistency of style, folk expressions and maxims were sometimes simplified and reworded without, however, changing their metaphorical content.

The above procedure yielded a final list of 108 basic-level metaphors (72 from books of maxims and thesauri, 22 from student generated slang expressions, and 14 from miscellaneous sources). No claim is made for the completeness of the list. Almost any definition, folk saying, or even adjectival modifier, involves some use of metaphor, in that one term is used to stand for, or elaborate upon the meaning of another. Nevertheless, we can say with some confidence that the final list is representative of the more common metaphors of hope. (Since all the metaphors will be presented below, readers may judge for themselves the accuracy of this assertion. Depending on personal preference and experience, some of the listed metaphors could be deleted, and others added. However, such deletions and additions would not change the thrust of the analysis.)

The next step in the analysis involved grouping the basic-level metaphors into broader, more abstract categories. The nature of this task did not lend itself well to formal procedures. The grouping required considerable discussion among the three judges, and repeated iterations were made until consensus was reached. Twenty-one middle-level categories were thus formed. These 21 middle-level categories were further grouped into 7 highly abstract metaphors, plus a miscellaneous category.

Results

Following the classification procedure described above, the 108 basic-level metaphors of hope were grouped into the following eight categories (seven abstract metaphors, plus a miscellaneous category). The number of basic-level metaphors in each category is listed in parentheses.

I. Hope is a vital principle. (27)
II. Hope is a source of light and warmth. (14)

   III. Hope is elevated in space. (14)
   IV. Hope is a form of support. (8)
    V. Hope is a physical object or thing. (21)
   VI. Hope is deception. (8)
  VII. Hope is pressure. (7)
 VIII. Miscellaneous metaphors. (9)

Categories I (hope is a vital principle) and V (hope is a physical object or thing) are the most productive, in the sense that they contain the largest number of basic-level metaphors. However, the mere counting of metaphors within a category can be misleading. For one thing, the categories are not independent; in many instances, a given basic-level metaphor could reasonably be placed in more than one higher- order category. Categories I through IV, in particular, have overlapping meanings. They form a superordinate grouping somewhat distinct from the remaining categories.

For another thing, the number of metaphors in a category is to some extent an artifact of language. For example, many different kinds of food are recognized in ordinary language, and there are different ways of preparing food. Hence, numerous lexical variations (basic-level metaphors) are possible on the theme that hope, like food, does (or does not) provide nourishment. By contrast, other metaphors (e.g., that hope is like a dream) allow little lexical variation, although they may be oft repeated. Unfortunately, the frequency of usage of a metaphor in ordinary language cannot be easily ascertained and is not reflected in the mere count of the number of metaphors contained within a category. As a rough guideline, however, it is safe to assume that the more conventionalized a metaphor has become, the more frequently it finds expression in everyday discourse.

In the final analysis, the importance or productivity of a metaphor has less to do with the number of lexical variations on a theme, or with the frequency of usage, as with the richness of the metaphor's implications, e.g., the transfer of knowledge from the source to the target domain. In this respect, idiosyncratic metaphors are frequently more productive than conventional metaphors.

Let us turn now to a complete listing of the basic-level metaphors of hope, organized by categories (abstract metaphors).

I. Hope is a vital principle

A. Hope is the basis of life
1. Hope is the balm and life blood of the soul.
2. Hope is the second soul of the unhappy.
3. Where there's life there's hope.
4. Hope springs eternal in the human breast.
5. Alive with hope.
6. Never say "die."
7. Without hope the heart would break.

B. Hope is food (but not always nourishing)
1. Hope is the poor man's bread.
2. Hope is a good breakfast but an ill supper.
3. Hope is a poor salad to dine and sup with.
4. Hope is a good sauce but poor food.
5. He who lives on hope will die fasting.
6. They that feed upon hope may be said to hang on, but not to live.

C. Hope is a remedy for what ails a person
1. The miserable have no other medicine but hope.
2. Hope and patience are the two sovereign remedies for all.
3. Of all ills that men endure, hope is the only cheap and universal cure.
4. Hope is a charm for every woe.
5. Hope supports the afflicted.
6. Hope gives you strength.
7. The sickening pang of hope deferred.

D. Hope is an environmental condition conducive to life.
1. The springtime of hope.
2. In the land of hope there is never any winter.

3. Hope is like a downpour after a drought.

E. Hope is itself a form of life
   1. Nourish hope.
   2. Foster hope.
   3. Nurse hope.
   4. Keep hope alive.

By any standard, hope as a vital principle is the most productive of the abstract metaphors. It has many extensions (subcategories) and lexical variations, including some common, everyday expressions. For example, hope may be identified with a *life principle* (e.g., as the *life blood of the soul*). An extension of this life-sustaining theme is that hope is *food* or a *remedy for ailments*; so, too, is the identification of hope with *environmental conditions* (e.g., *springtime*) associated with the renewal of life. Finally, there is a set of conventional metaphors in which hope is itself treated as a *life form*, to be "nourished," "fostered," and the like. These latter expressions have become so much a part of our common language that their metaphorical implications may at first pass unnoticed.

The general implication of this class of metaphors is that hope is a kind of force or energy, a *vis vitalis*. Other emotions, such as anger and love (Kovecses, 1986, 1988), also draw on force or energy metaphors. The implication, however, is somewhat different, at least in the case of anger. Anger is often depicted as a kind of *pressure* or *explosive energy*. Hope, by contrast, is more like potential than kinetic energy. A person is sustained, not driven, by hope. Love falls between these two extremes, sometimes being depicted as a *driving force*, and sometimes as a *source of sustenance*.

A certain ambivalence toward hope can also be detected in these metaphors, especially those comparing hope to food. Hope may be good at the outset (a *good breakfast, but a poor supper*); it may complement a meal (as a *salad* or *sauce*); but it is not sufficient by itself to sustain life in a healthy fashion. This ambivalence about hope is even more evident in some of the other categories to be discussed below (especially Category VI, hope is deception). The ambivalence stems, in part, from the fact (noted in connection with Study 1) that hope is vain or foolish if it fosters unrealistic expectations, or lulls a person into inaction. Hope should assist, and not be a substitute for action.

II. Hope is a source of light and heat

    A. Hope is a sun or star
        1. A little sun must shine into everybody's life.
        2. Hopes are woven of sunbeams; a shadow annihilates them.
        3. Hope—that star of life's tremulous ocean.
        4. Every cloud has a silver lining.
        5. It's always darkest before the dawn.

    B. Hope is light
        1. There's a light at the end of the tunnel.
        2. Look at the bright side of life.
        3. A ray of hope.
        4. A glimmer of hope.

    C. If too intense, the light can blind
        1. Blinded by hope.

    D. Hope is fire
        1. Warmed by hope, frozen by dread.
        2. Consumed by hope.
        3. Glow with hope.

    E. The fire (light) can go out
        1. Hope extinguished.

This set of metaphors is closely related to the first (hope as a vital principle) in that both presuppose a notion of energy. In the present case, however, the source of energy is external to the individual—more like the *sun* than the *life blood of the soul.* The sun is, of course, necessary for life, but it serves other functions as well. For example, the sun gives off both light and heat. As *light*, hope can brighten the way, lead one out of darkness, and so forth. But it can also blind. As *heat*, hope may help "thaw" or animate behavior; or, if too intense, it may consume the individual.

The implications of this abstract metaphor would seem to be both literary and explanatory. On the literary side, expressions such as "light," "bright," and "warm," convey a positive or happy mood. On the explanatory side, such metaphors allow more precise inferences about the nature and functions of hope. For example, to the extent that hopes are *woven of sunbeams*, they are insubstantial and ephemeral. More generally, however, light has a guiding function; it gives (or allows) direction. With hope, one need not wander in darkness, nor be paralyzed ("frozen") by dread.

III. Hope is elevated in space

A. Hope is "up"
1. Hope is an instinct which we cannot repress, and which lifts us up.
2. Hope elevates, and joy brightens his crest.
3. Have high hopes.
4. Reach for the sky (or stars).
5. Keep your spirits up.
6. Raise hopes.

B. Hope flies, like a bird
1. Hope: The natural flights of the human mind.
2. Let your spirits soar.
3. On the wings of hope.

C. What is in the air lacks substantial support
1. The houses hope builds are castles in the air.
2. Pie in the sky.
3. On cloud nine.

D. Reality brings you back to earth
1. His hopes were shot down.
2. Come back down to earth.
3. Get your feet back on the ground.

Spatial metaphors are among the most common in academic as well as popular psychology. Gentner and Grudin (1985) suggest that this may be due to the fact that "perceptual space is among our most familiar and best understood areas of well-structured knowledge" (p. 188). For whatever reason, space lends itself well to both literary and explanatory metaphors. An upward location in space generally conveys a positive image. Heaven (or its equivalent in most cultures) is up; hell is down. A person who is happy is "higher than a kite." A person in control is "on top of things." To inspire is to "uplift." And so forth. In keeping with its generally positive connotation, hope is also given an upward direction in space. There is, however, more to this metaphor than simply the connotation of being *up*. There is also the implication that with hope a person can "rise to the task." In other words, this is a variation on the theme, emphasized in Category I, that hope sustains.

An extension of this metaphor is the notion that hope allows a person to *fly*, even *soar, like a bird*. In fact, a bird on the wing is a common representation of hope in visual arts as well as in poetry. On the negative side, "what is up must come down." This is as true of hope as it is of anything else. Other than wings, there may be little to support hope's elevated position. Hence, hope may be less like a soaring bird than a *pie in the sky*, or a *castle in the air*. And even birds can be *shot down*.

In short, the basic implication of this group of metaphors would seem to be not only that hope is uplifting, but that it can also be fleeting and without foundation.

IV. Hope is a form of support

    A. Hope is an underpinning
        1. Rest on hope.
        2. Buoyed up by hope.
        3. Hope will carry you through.
        4. Hope and patience are the softest cushions to lean on in adversity.

B. Hope is a prop
  1. Hope is a lover's staff.
  2. Hope is a rope.
  3. Cling to hope.

C. The prop may be insubstantial
  1. Hope is a slender reed for a stout man to lean on.
  2. Grasping at straws.

This set of metaphors is a corollary of the former (Category III). That is, to the extent that hope "lifts us up," it implies some form of support. Even when a person is firmly on the ground, support may be necessary, e.g., to hold oneself upright, to lean against, to rest on, and so forth. The metaphor of hope as a form of support is also related to the metaphor of hope as a vital principle (Category I). In both instances, the implication is that hope helps to sustain the individual, albeit in somewhat different ways.

Desroche (1979) introduced his sociological study of hope by reference to a metaphor from this class: *Hope is a rope* ("*die Hoffnung ist ein Seil*"), attributed to the 17th century German mystic, Angelus Silesius. As Desroche points out, in many mystical traditions the fakir or shaman throws a rope in the air (or, alternatively, the rope may fall from the sky). Although the rope appears to be attached to nothing substantial, it nevertheless holds fast, allowing the fakir to ascend.

Desroche believes this metaphor reflects something basic about human nature, namely, the "constitutive imagination." Human beings, held down by the weight of necessities, find something like a rope by which they can ascend to a higher plane. "To the observer, it seems that there is nothing to keep it [the rope] up, except for the impalpable and inconsistent worlds of fantasy, wanderings and absurdity" (p. 3). Like the rope of the fakir, hope also defies the gravity of the everyday world, and allows the individual to ascend to a higher plane of reality.

V. Hope is a physical object or thing

A. Hope is an object of value
1. Hope is the best possession. None are completely wretched but those who are without hope; and few are reduced so low as that.
2. He that wants hope, is the poorest man alive.
3. A good Hope is better than a bad possession.
4. Hope is worth any money.

B. Hope is an object to be safeguarded
1. Guard one's hopes.
2. Cherish hope.

C. Hope is a gift or offering
1. Give hope.
2. Hold out hope to.
3. Offer hope.

D. At certain times, hope should be/is discarded
1. Give up all hope.
2. Abandon all hope.
3. Reject hope.
4. Relinquish hope.

E. A person may temporarily be without hope
1. Have no hope.
2. Destitute of hope.
3. Out of hope.
4. Lose all hope.

F. Hope may be regained
1. Find hope.
2. Recover hope.

G. Hope is a fragile object
1. Dash someone's hopes.
2. Shatter someone's hopes.

The identification of hope with a **physical object** is another very productive (abstract) metaphor, in the sense that it has numerous extensions and lexical variations. To a certain extent, this productivity reflects the fact that the notion of an **object** or **thing** is very general; hence, much can be encompassed by the metaphor. But that is not all there is to it. Note that most of the basic-level metaphors in this category are highly conventionalized. That is, they consist of short phrases that have become a part of everyday speech (e.g., to *offer hope*). This suggests a high frequency of use.

Metaphors of this class carry the objectivation of hope to its extreme. The major implication is that hope is an entity that can be completely separated from the individual. Hope can thus be *lost, found, given, received,* and so forth. Put another way, hope is something a person has (or doesn't have); it is not something a person does.

The value of hope is also emphasized by this set of metaphors. Hope is a *possession* to be prized; to be *destitute of hope* is among the worst of all possible conditions. This positive view of hope stands in stark contrast to the negative aspects of hope described in the next group of metaphors.

VI. Hope is deception

A. Hope is a person who deceives
 1. Hope is generally a poor guide, but very good company along the way.
 2. Hope is the only liar who never loses his reputation for veracity.
 3. Hope is a charlatan who always defrauds us.
 4. Hope is a traitor of the mind; under color of friendship, it robs us of resolution.

B. Hope is self-deception
 1. It is natural for a person to indulge in the illusions of hope.
 2. Hope is a pathological belief in the occur rence of the impossible.

3. Hope is what dreams are made of.

C. Hope obscures your vision
   1. Hope can cloud your eyes.

The implication of this group of metaphors is obvious: Hope can deceive and lead a person astray. Whereas the previous category (hope is a **physical object**) focused almost exclusively on the positive aspects of hope (e.g., as a *valuable possession*), the present category emphasizes the negative. There also are metaphors that attribute to hope beneficial guiding qualities, but these have been included in Category II (cf. hope as *light*).

VII. Hope is pressure

A. Hope is a gas confined under pressure
   1. Full of hope.
   2. Bursting with hope.

B. If the container explodes, the gas escapes
   1. His balloon burst.

C. If the gas is released, the container collapses.
   1. He had all the air knocked out of him.
   2. He was crushed.

D. The pressure performs useful work.
   1. Hope swells my sail.
   2. Hope: The spur to industry.

This is the final category that can be taken to represent a single abstract metaphor. It is a minor and somewhat heterogeneous category. However, it accrues special interest from the fact that, of all the metaphors of hope, it comes closest to the principle metaphor of anger, as described by Kovecses (1986; Lakoff & Kovecses, 1983): Anger is the heat of a fluid in a container. Indeed, in one variation or another, this abstract metaphor would be applicable to a wide variety of different emotions (Averill, in press b; Kovecses, 1986, 1988).

According to Kovecses, when the intensity (heat) of the anger increases, the fluid rises (wells up), increasing the pressure in the container (the person), until he or she loses control (blows up). Hope, too, may fill a person to the point of bursting. The connotation is, however, somewhat different than in the case of anger. Anger is like a liquid that boils, seethes, steams, stews, and the like. Hope is more like a *gas;* it has an airy, ephemeral quality. The container which is filled with hope is like a balloon, as opposed to a pot or kettle that might hold a boiling liquid. Balloons are light; they rise and may even lift things up. The gas in a balloon also helps to sustain its shape. Thus, the container may not only burst if the internal pressure becomes too great, but it also will collapse or be crushed if there is insufficient pressure (not enough hope).

Finally, the pressure of a gas can be put to useful work, even when it is not contained. The *wind in a sail* is a good example. More generally, hope can be a *spur or impetus to industry.*

VIII. Miscellaneous metaphors

> Hope is grief's best music.
> Hope sings the tune without the words and never stops.
> Prisoner of hope.
> Counting chickens before they hatch.
> Take heart.
> Hope is as cheap as despair.
> Work without hope draws nectar in a sieve.
> Fair hope, with smiling face but ling'ring foot.
> A mask the dying person wears.

This category does not represent a single abstract metaphor, and many of the entries have something in common with the previous groupings. They are presented primarily for the sake of completeness.

Discussion: Rules and Parameters of Hope

We have provided brief discussions of the major abstract metaphors of hope as they were presented. We will therefore organize this more general discussion around the two main issues addressed in Study 1 (the general principles or rules of hope) and Study 2 (the criteria for classifying hope as an emotion).

The Rules of Hope

We have drawn many of the metaphors of hope from maxims and proverbs. Not surprisingly, therefore, they frequently contain prescriptions and warnings regarding the appropriate occasions for, and the proper expression of hope.

Prudential rules. Warning against imprudent hope can be found in most of the abstract categories that we have delineated. For example, hope can be *good sauce but poor food* (I), a person can be *blinded* by hope (II); hope is a *pie in the sky* (III), a *slender reed* (IV), a *charlatan* (VI), or even more explicitly, a *pathological belief* in the occurrence of the impossible (VI). These negative metaphors may be contrasted with the more positive ones, in which hope is compared, for example, to the *life blood of the soul* (I), a *guiding star* (II), a *soft cushion* (IV), or a *valuable possession* (V). The positive metaphors presumably refer to prudent as opposed to foolish or vain hopes. The implication of these metaphors would seem to be that hope is valuable primarily to the extent that it is realistic.

Moralistic rules. It is often difficult (and somewhat arbitrary) to distinguish moralistic from prudential rules, since both exhort the individual to be wise rather than foolish. The fact that hope has long been considered a major virtue attests to the moral as well as the prudential connotation of many of the metaphors of hope. For example, persons would not be encouraged to *nourish* and *cherish* hopes that lead to immoral acts. Conversely, the characterization of hope as form of deception can serve as a warning against immoral as well as imprudent behavior.

Priority rules. The results of Study 1 suggested that a person may hope for almost anything within the bounds set by prudential and moralistic rules—provided the event is sufficiently important. This latter stipulation is what we mean by priority rules; that is, hope should be about matters of consequence. Priority rules are reflected in the importance often attributed to hope itself. This is particularly evident in the metaphors of Category I, hope as a vital principle. Consider, for example, the metaphorical connection between hope and medicine. Aside from the curative properties of hope implied by this metaphor, there is also an implicit injunction: A person should take medicine only when needed, or else it may do more harm than good. A somewhat similar lesson can be learned from the comparison between hope and food. A person should beware of "junk hope" as much as of junk food.

Action rules. Of the 108 metaphors examined in the present study, very few refer to specific responses that the hopeful individual could or should make. In a study of the metaphors of anger, by contrast, Lakoff and Kovecses (1983) mention 164 metaphors, roughly one- third of which refer to such responses as: agitated behavior (e.g., blowing up, hitting the ceiling, having a fit, flipping one's lid); aggressive acts (e.g., snarling, glowering, looking daggers, tearing one's hair out); and/or physiological change (e.g., getting a hernia, bursting a blood vessel, breathing fire, becoming flushed or blue in the face). Similarly, many of the metaphors of love refer to behavioral tendencies and/or physiological reactions (Kovecses, 1988).

The fact that few metaphors of hope refer to specific responses is consistent with the results of Study 2. It may be recalled that when subjects were asked to distinguish hope from anger and love, the most frequently mentioned difference was that hope is less demonstrable (see Table 2.1). Nevertheless, many metaphors of hope do refer to action or striving in general. Thus, people should *never say die* (I); on the contrary, they should *reach for the sky* (III). Hope is also *a spur to industry* (VII), and without hope *work draws nectar from a sieve* (VIII).

In sum, the rules of hope identified on the basis of subjects' responses to questionnaires in Study 1 are also embodied in the metaphors of hope found in ordinary language. Of course, the metaphors of hope are more than simply exhortations about how to think and behave; they also speak to the ontology of hope as conceived of in ordinary language. We will examine next one aspect of that ontology, namely, the features of hope that lead it to be classified as an emotion.

Emotional Parameters

In Study 2, we identified a number of parameters of the emotional model through a comparison of hope to anger and love. To keep the present discussion within limits, we will consider the following five features from Table 2.1: (a) hope, anger and love are all difficult to control; (b) all affect the way you think or perceive events, e.g., in obsessional, irrational, or illusory ways; (c) all affect the way you behave, e.g., leading you to act in different or unusual ways; (e) all motivate behavior, increase persistence, enable one to go on; and (e) all are common or universal experiences. Excluding the categorization of hope as an emotion and/or feeling, these five features were the most frequently mentioned similarities among hope, anger, and love reported by subjects in Study 2.

(a) *Hope is difficult to control.* As discussed in connection with Study 2, a lack of personal control is one of the most important criteria for classifying a response as emotional. Emotions are passions (things that happen to us) and not actions (things we do). In all eight categories of metaphors that we have distinguished, there are at least a few basic-level metaphors that imply passivity or a lack of personal control. Thus, hope *springs eternal in the human breast* (I); if too intense, it can *consume* a person (II); or, under more favorable conditions, it can *lift one up* (III) and *carry one through* (IV). Like a thing separate from the self, hope can also be *lost, found, abandoned,* etc. (V). Hope is also a *charlatan who always defrauds us* (VI). Finally, a person may *burst* from too much hope (VII), or even be a *prisoner of hope* (VIII).

In short, the metaphors of our language clearly place hope among the passions.

(b) *Hope affects the way a person thinks* and/or (c) *behaves.* These two features (related to cognition and behavior, respectively) can best be considered together, for they touch upon a similar theme, namely, the presumed irrationality, or at least nonrationality, of hope. As discussed in connection with Study 2, this theme is also closely linked to the previous one (hope as a passion). Behavior that is not rational is often considered beyond control.

As we saw in the earlier discussion of prudential rules, a theme of irrationality is common in many of the negative metaphors of hope (see especially Category VI, hope is deception). But even when hope is considered prudent, it may still be regarded as nonrational (as opposed to irrational). A hope, like a dream, need not follow the rules of logic. In general, emotional beliefs are judged in terms of appropriateness, not in terms of truth value. Hope is clearly no exception (cf. the hope of a parent for the recovery of a fatally ill child).

(d) *Hope motivates behavior.* This feature is perhaps most evident in the metaphors of Category VII (hope is pressure), which reflects an energy model of motivation (e.g., hope *swells one's sails*). Many of the metaphors of Categories I through IV (i.e., hope as a vital principle, a source of light and heat, elevated in space, and a form of support) also have a motivational connotation. In these instances, however, the "energy" of hope is more like that found in food than like the pressure exerted by a gusty wind. In other words, hope can not only propel one to action; as importantly, it can *nourish, warm, uplift,* and *support* an individual in situations where no direct action is possible.

(e) *Hope is a common or universal experience.* This feature is reflected primarily in the metaphors of Category I (hope is a vital principle). Hope, as the *balm and life blood of the soul,* is almost equated with life itself. Indeed, *where there is life there is hope* is a very common expression. If by "hope," we mean simply a tendency to adopt positive outlook, or persuade oneself that what is desired will come to pass, then hope is undoubtedly a universal and even necessary part of life (cf. Tiger, 1979). But such biases are probably better labeled optimism than hope. It remains to be determined whether hope *as an emotion* is a universal experience.

To summarize briefly, the experience of hope as reported by subjects in Studies 1 and 2 generally conforms to cultural expectations as found in proverbs, maxims, and metaphors (Study 3). This is an important point, for it means that the results reported in Chapters 1 and 2 are not restricted to the sample of subjects used in those studies. It also suggests one of the ways that emotions are acquired during socialization. As a child acquires language, he or she automatically incorporates many of the distinctions and rules (i.e., the "implicit theories") by which emotions are constituted. Metaphorically speaking, language is the "mother's milk" of emotional development.

IV

Study 4:
Cross-Cultural Variations

In the introduction, we noted how the concept—and presumably the experience—of hope has undergone change during the course of Western history. For example, hope (*elpis*) was regarded primarily as a negative state by the Greeks, but as a major virtue by later Christians. There is also evidence that hope is constituted differently, at least in its emotional connotation, across cultures today. In constructing a cross-cultural lexicon of emotional concepts, Boucher (1980) asked informants from various countries to name as many emotions as they could; a week was generally allowed for the task. "Hope" (or its near equivalent in the indigenous languages) was mentioned by informants from the United States, Australia, Puerto Rico, and Japan. Informants from Korea, Indonesia, Malaysia, and Sri Lanka did not mention hope among the emotions of their cultures.

The purpose of this fourth study was to explore the meaning of hope both in the United States, where hope is counted among the emotions, and in Korea, where it is not. The Koreans do have a term, *himang*, that is typically translated as "hope"; and, as we shall see shortly, *himang* has most of the usual connotations of hope, at least in a cognitive sense. How is *himang* conceptualized among the Koreans, if not as an emotional state? And do the rules of hope, as identified for Americans, also apply to Koreans? These are among the questions addressed by the present study.

Method

Questionnaire

The questionnaire used in the present study was similar to that used in Study 1. However, some of the items were worded differently, and other items were added or deleted to fit the cross-cultural context. An initial English version of the questionnaire was translated into Korean by one of the authors, who is a native Korean. Following a back translation, some portions of the English version were changed in order to be as equivalent to the Korean as possible.

In all cases (both Korean and American), instructions for completing the questionnaire were delivered primarily in writing.

Subjects

Subjects were 100 students (68 males and 32 females) at Sungkyunkwan University in Seoul[1], and 100 students (35 males and 65 females) at the University of Massachusetts, Amherst. The questionnaire was administered to the Korean subjects during regularly scheduled class periods. Two classes

---

[1] Universities in Korea are very competitive. There are about 100 four-year colleges and universities across the nation of 40 million people, Sungkyunkwan University is regarded as one of the five best institutes in Korea.

were used: one in Industrial Psychology (n = 51), and the other in Educational Psychology (n = 49). One group of American subjects also completed the questionnaire during an industrial psychology class (n = 37). A second group (n = 32) was recruited from a course in Personality Psychology; in this case, the students took the questionnaire home and returned it a subsequent class period. Finally, a third group of American subjects (n = 31) was recruited from a variety of different psychology courses, and the questionnaire was administered in small group sessions.

Analyses were performed to assess whether any systematic biases were introduced by the various recruitment procedures. The two groups of Korean subjects (from the Industrial and Educational Psychology courses) yielded very similar results. So, too, did the three groups of American subjects. Therefore, scores were combined within each culture to yield a single Korean sample and a single American sample.[2]

The average age of subjects in the Korean sample was 22.1 years (range, 18 to 29); 24% were sophomores, 73% juniors, and 3% seniors. The average age of the American sample was 20.9 years (range, 19 to 34); 15% were sophomores, 35% juniors, and 49% seniors (one American did not indicate a grade).[3] All the data were collected during the same Fall Semester. Preliminary analyses indicated no confounding due to age or grade level.

There was a marked sex imbalance among the samples, with 68% of the Koreans being male but only 35% of the Americans. It may be recalled that no reliable sex

---

[2] Originally the Korean sample consisted of 103 subjects and the American sample of 104. However, for ease of presentation (to make the number of subjects responding to an item equal to the percentage), and to reduce the imbalance in sex ratios, each sample was reduced to 100 subjects by randomly eliminating three males form the original Korean sample and four females from the American sample.

[3] The age of Korean students is generally higher than that of their American counterparts, partly because Korean students tend to finish their compulsory military service during their college years.

differences were observed in Study 1. Nevertheless, as a precautionary measure, sex was included whenever appropriate as a factor in the analysis of data. Few significant effects were observed, and none interacted with the cross-cultural comparisons presented below. Therefore, possible sex differences are not discussed further.

Results

The results are presented in two sections: the first compares Korean and American views on the nature of hope in general; and the second analyses specific, representative episodes of hope from both cultures.

General Conceptualizations of Hope

Under this heading, we will consider three types of data: the categorization of hope; synonyms and antonyms of hope; and the relationship of hope to fantasy.

The categorization of hope. Subjects were first asked to rate the extent to which hope belongs to each of 10 basic psychological categories (e.g., an emotion, an intellectual process, an attitude). Ratings were made on three point scales (0 = not at all, 1 = somewhat, 2 = very much). The mean ratings for each categorization were compared by two-way analyses of variance, with culture and sex as independent variables (see Table 4.1).

The data in Table 4.1 can be looked at in two ways: first, in terms of absolute differences in ratings (as reflected in the F-ratios); and, second, in terms of rank order. With regard to absolute differences, Americans gave significantly higher ratings to hope as a "way of coping" and as a "feeling" than did the Koreans. There was no significant difference in the ratings of hope as an "emotion"; however, this category ranked third for the Americans, and sixth for the Koreans, indicating that its connotation in the hierarchy was different for the two groups.

In contrast to the Americans, Koreans gave significantly higher ratings to hope as a "personality characteristic,"

Table 4.1. Mean ratings (and rank order) of hope (himang) by American and Korean subjects.

Category	Mean rating[a] (rank) US	Korea	Significance F	Probability
A way of coping (e.g., with a handicap)	1.74 (1)	1.46 (4)	8.18	<.01
A feeling	1.72 (2)	1.17 (8)	43.25	<.01
An emotion	1.42 (3)	1.34 (6)	.64	ns
An attitude	1.31 (4)	1.24 (7)	.57	ns
A voluntary process	1.26 (5)	1.64 (1.5)	19.67	<.01
A personality characteristic	1.18 (6.5)	1.64 (1.5)	26.02	<.01
A socially acquired motive	1.18 (6.5)	1.60 (3)	19.73	<.01
A biologically based need	.84 (8)	.89 (9)	.93	ns
An intellectual process	.83 (9)	1.40 (5)	27.39	<.01
An involuntary process	.69 (10)	.58 (10)	.56	ns

[a]0 = not at all; 1 = somewhat; 2 = very much

a "voluntary process," a "socially acquired motive," and an "intellectual process." Each of these categorizations would seem to differentiate hope from emotions in general, at least as emotions are typically conceived of in Western cultures.

Some of the differences in Table 4.1 may reflect subtle differences in the categories listed, as well as in the meaning of hope. For example, the English term, "emotion," can be translated as either chongso or kamchong. We chose chongso, since that is the term commonly used in Korean psychology textbooks. We used the other term (kamchong) as a translation for "feeling." However, in everyday speech and popular literature, kamchong is often used in a sense roughly equivalent to "emotion," and some of the subjects in this study may have interpreted it so. Needless to say, similar considerations apply to the English terms, "feeling" and "emotion," which are often used interchangeably in popular discourse. For cross-cultural comparison, the two categories should probably be combined into a single "feeling/emotion" category. If such a combination is made, the difference between Korean and American conceptions of hope becomes even more pronounced.

Synonyms and antonyms of hope. A concept derives its meaning, in part, from other concepts with which it is similar and from which it differs. At the end of the questionnaire subjects were asked to name three synonyms and three antonyms of hope. The Americans listed 263 different synonyms and 244 antonyms; the Koreans listed the same number of synonyms and antonyms—288 in both cases. The terms listed by five or more subjects in each culture are presented in Table 4.2.

In both cultures, hope is regarded as similar to a wish, desire, need, want, dream, and/or expectation. But there are also noticeable differences between cultures. Americans counted as synonyms such terms as faith, prayer, belief, feeling, and trust; by contrast, Koreans saw hope as related to ideal, ambition, pursuit, success, effort, and goal. The difference in connotation between these two clusters of terms is evident. The mention of faith, prayer, etc., by Americans probably reflects the influence of the Judeo-Christian religious tradition, where hope is regarded as a major virtue (along with faith and charity). Analogously, the Korean responses may reflect the influence of Confucianism. As will be explained more fully in a subsequent section, Confucianism emphasizes the ideal person and society. The desire to achieve these ideals may help explain why so many Koreans listed ambition, effort, and pursuit as synonyms of hope.

With regard to antonyms, both groups considered despair, pessimism, giving up, discouragement and realism as opposites of hope. The Americans also emphasized indifference, apathy, and a lack of caring or concern, whereas frustration and failure were commonly mentioned by the Koreans. These differences are consistent with the American emphasis on faith and trust, and the Korean emphasis on ambition and effort. Faith that is thwarted leads to indifference; effort that is thwarted leads to frustration.

Distinguishing hope from fantasy. To distinguish hope from merely wishing or desiring something, subjects were asked to describe three things that might make life easier and more enjoyable, but that they should not hope for. (Henceforth, these will be referred to as *fantasy objects*.) Subjects also were asked to describe the reasons that they should not

Table 4.2. Synonyms and antonyms of hope as mentioned by American and Korean subjects.

Synonyms		Antonyms	
American	Korean[a]	American	Korean[a]
Wish(52)	Wish(*Paraem;Somang* 57)[b]	Despair(31)	Despair(*Cholmang* 46)
Desire(50)	Dream(*Kkum* 31)	Pessimism(26)	Frustration(*Chwajol* 39)
Faith(32)	Expectation(*Kidae* 17)	Giving up(11)	Giving up(*P'ogi* 30)
Want(30)	Desire(*Yongmang* 13)	Uncaring(11)	Discouragement(*Nakdam* 13)
Optimism(25)	Longing(*Sowon* 8)	Indifferent(10)	Failure(*Shilp'ae* 10)
Prayer(16)	Ideal(*Isang* 7)	Apathy(8)	Desperation(*Nangmang* 9)
Dream(14)	Want(*Wonham* 6)	Depression(8)	Dissatisfaction(*P'ulman* 7)
Belief(9)	Ambition(*P'obu* 6)	Realism(8)	Pessimism(*P'igwan* 6)
Need(8)	Pursuit(*Ch'ugu* 6)	Disbelief(7)	Disappointment(*Shilmang* 5)
Positive(7)	Need(*Yokgu* 6)	Discouragement(7)	Realism(*Hyonshil* 5)
Expectation(6)	Success(*Songong* 5)	Negative(7)	Self-abandonment(*Chap'ojagi* 5)
Feeling(7)	Aspire(*Yolmang* 5)	Desire(5)	
Trust(5)	Effort(*Noryok* 5)	Faithlessness(5)	
	Goal(*Mokp'yo* 5)	Unconcerned(5)	

Note.–Each subject (100 Americans and 100 Koreans) mentioned up to three synonyms and antonyms. The numbers in parentheses represent the frequency with which a term was mentioned. Only terms mentioned by five or or more subjects are listed.

[a]Korean responses were Romanized based on the ROK Ministry of Education version (1984) of standardization.

[b]"Wish" seems to be an equally appropriate translation of both *Paraem* and *Somang*. *Paraem*, which is indigenous Korean, was mentioned by 37 subjects; *Somang*, which is a derivative of Chinese, was mentioned by 20 subjects.

hope for the realization of each fantasy. The answers to both open-ended questions were analyzed following procedures similar to those used in Study 1. That is, three judges first categorized the data independently. A common set of categories was then derived, and the responses were again sorted, using this new set of categories. Each response was repeatedly discussed until the judges reached agreement.

Ten categories of fantasy objects were finally agreed upon, plus a miscellaneous category. These are presented in Table 4.3. For Americans, the most frequently mentioned fantasies involved material goods (e.g., money, car), interpersonal relationships (e.g., meeting friends), and achievement (e.g., success in academic endeavors). For Koreans, the most frequent fantasies involved hedonistic pursuits (e.g., sex, food), material goods (e.g., money), and freedom from social and personal obligations (e.g., doing whatever one wants).

Table 4.3. Objects that would make life easier or more enjoyable, but for which subjects believed they should not hope.

Fantasy object	Percent (rank) US	Korea	Probability[a]
Material goods (e.g., money, car)	32% (1)	16% (2)	<.01
Interpersonal relationships (e.g., meeting friends, improved family relations, getting married)	15% (2)	6% (6)	<.01[b]
Achievement: short-term (e.g., passing an exam)	14% (3)	5% (8)	<.01
Change in personal characteristics (e.g., health)	9% (4)	1% (9.5)	<.01[b]
Happiness and well-being (e.g., comfort)	8% (5)	6% (6)	ns
Leisure activity (e.g., travel)	3% (6.5)	1% (9.5)	ns
Achievement: long-term (e.g., a new career)	3% (6.5)	6% (6)	ns
Freedom from social and personal obligations (e.g., in order to do what one wants)	2% (8)	15% (3)	<.01
Hedonistic pursuits (e.g., sex)	2% (9.5)	17% (1)	<.01
Social status (e.g., power)	2% (9.5)	8% (4)	<.01

Note.–Each subject listed up to three objects.   Results are presented as percentages of the total number of objects: American responses, n = 258; Korean responses, n = 278. (11% of the American and 19% of the Korean responses were unclassifiable.)

[a]Probability levels are based on the chi-square statistic, using all responses.

[b]When only the initial response of each subject was used (thus preserving independence of observation, but greatly reducing the number of observations) group differences were not statistically significant (p > .05) for these variables.

Of greater interest than the objects of fantasy are the reasons why subjects did not hope for these objects. The reasons are presented in Table 4.4. For comparative purposes, Table 4.4 is organized according to the four types of norms (prudential, moralistic, priority, and action rules) identified in Studies 1 and 2.[4]

Both Americans and Koreans frequently mentioned practical reasons (prudential rules) for not hoping. There was, however, a difference in emphasis. The Americans tended to focus on the impossibility of achieving the objects of their fantasies, whereas the Koreans focused on potential disadvantage effects should their fantasies be realized. The Koreans (by a ratio of almost four to one) also expressed more concern than did the Americans about the violation of social and/or personal values (moralistic rules).

The data in Table 4.4 also suggest that Americans view the relation of hope to action somewhat differently than do the Koreans. The nature of the differences are not, however, immediately obvious. We have seen how Koreans regard hope as a voluntary response (see Table 4.1), synonymous in some respects to ambition and pursuit (Table 4.2). Clearly, then, hope is associated with action for Koreans as well as for Americans (see also Table 4.5, below). The main difference seems to lie in the nature of the association. For Americans, hope is closely related to faith (in one form or another). There is always the danger, therefore, that instead of encouraging effort, hope may serve as a substitute for action. As we saw in Study 3, many of the metaphors of hope warn against such a possibility. It is a warning echoed by many of the American subjects in the present study: Hope should not be a substitute for work.

---

[4] Since the rules are based on American norms, their applicability to a Korean sample might be questioned. And, in fact, there is reason to believe that the rules are not directly transferrable. For example, in both America and Korea, hope is related to action, but the rules of action appear to be somewhat different in the two cultures. Nevertheless, the rules are stated in such general terms that they can be used heuristically (if cautiously) without undue distortion of the data.

Table 4.4. Reasons for not hoping, categorized according to the norms (rules) of hope.

Reasons for not hoping	Percent (rank) US	Korea	Probability[a]
Prudential norms			
Object is impossible or unrealistic.	28% (1)	12% (3)	<.01
Object would be impractical or disadvantageous; it is short-sighted; interfere with other, more pressing obligations.	9% (4)	21% (2)	<.01
Moralistic norms			
Object goes against personal and/or social values; is socially unacceptable; violates personal ideals.	10% (3)	37% (1)	<.01
Objects is damaging to, or goes against desires of family; fails to meet family obligations.	1% (9)	4% (5)	<.05[b]
Priority norms			
Objects lacks true worth or importance; it is not really wanted; one can do without it.	7% (5)	4% (5)	ns
Action norms			
Hope won't make it happen; one must work for the object.	15% (2)	0% (8)	<.01
Object will or will not happen naturally; one has no control over it.	4% (6.5)	0% (8)	<.01[b]
Can achieve the object through one's own efforts or hard work; one has control over it.	4% (6.5)	0% (8)	<.01[b]
Object would lose value if one didn't work for it; object must be achieved through one's own efforts.	2% (8)	4% (5)	ns

Note.--Each subject listed up to three reasons. The total number of reasons were 258 for Americans and 278 for Koreans. (20% of the American and 18% of the Korean responses were unclassifiable.)

[a]Probability levels are based on the chi-square statistic, using all responses.

[b]When only the initial response of each subject was used (thus preserving independence of observation, but greatly reducing the number of observations) group differences were not statistically significant (p >.05) for these variables.

At this point, a possible source of confounding should be considered with respect to the results presented in Table 4.4. Americans and Koreans tended to fantasize about different objects (see Table 4.3); perhaps the differences in reasons for not hoping simply reflect differences in the type of objects. For example, if Koreans more often fantasize about hedonistic pursuits (as they apparently do) and Americans about material objects (as they apparently do), then it might be expected that personal and social rules would be of greater concern for the Koreans, and pragmatic considerations of more importance for the Americans. Inspection of the data indicated, however, that the Koreans tended to focus on personal and social values as reasons for not hoping, regardless of the type of fantasy object; the Americans also were relatively consistent in their focus on practical concerns as salient reasons for not hoping.

Representative Episodes of Hope

The kind of data presented in the previous section may be inordinately influenced by stereotypical conceptions of hope. Therefore, subjects also were asked to describe a more specific, representative episode of hope, one that had begun (but not necessarily ended) during the past year.[5]

Preliminary analyses. There were no reliable differences between Americans and Koreans in the reported intensity of the episodes, in the perceived importance of the objects hoped for, nor in self-reported changes in mood from before to after the subject started hoping. Koreans did, however, tend to select episodes that were more enduring than did the Americans. For example, Koreans rated their episodes as "longer term" than did the Americans (mean of

---

[5] It will be recalled that in Study 1 subjects were asked to pick an episode that not only began but also *ended* within the year. Consistent with this difference between the two studies, the incidents described by American subjects in Study 4 were rated as significantly more important (8.8 vs 8.1, p <.05) and intense (7.9 vs 6.8, p <.01) than those reported in Study 1.

7.9 vs 6.8 on an 11-point scale, with 0 = "short-term" and 10 = "long-term," $F(1,196) = 7.59$, p <.01).

The remaining results concerning the representative episodes will be presented in three sections: (1) the type of events hoped for, (2) controllability of the event and probability of attainment, and (3) instrumental responses during hope.

Objects of hope. The open-ended descriptions of the representative episodes were categorized according to object (the type of event hoped for) by three judges, following the same procedure described above in connection with the fantasy objects. In this case, however, a fine-grained division was not attempted. Rather, we followed the categorization used in Study 1, with the addition of a new category ("ideal self and/or world") in order to accommodate the Korean data. The categories used, the percentage of American and Korean episodes falling within each category, and the p values for the significance of the differences between groups (based on a non-hierarchical log-linear analysis) are as follows: Achievement-related hopes (American, 34%; Korean, 48%; p < .01); hopes for improved interpersonal relationships (American, 24%; Korean 14%; n.s.); altruistic hopes (American, 16%; Korean, 2%; p < .01); hopes for an ideal self and/or world (American, 5%; Korean, 19%; p < .01); and miscellaneous hopes (American, 21%; Korean, 17%; n.s.).

For the most part, the above differences between groups are consistent with the results discussed earlier for hope in general. It will be recalled, for example, that a connotation of achievement characterized many of the synonyms of hope mentioned by the Koreans (see Table 4.2); hence, it is reasonable that the Koreans, more often than Americans, also selected representative episodes of hope that were achievement related.

The most marked difference between Americans and Koreans occurred with respect to altruistic hopes. This difference deserves special mention, lest it misinterpreted. In a broad sense, the episodes reported by the Koreans were as altruistic—if not more so—than those reported by the Americans. The difference lies primarily in the specificity of the events described. In the case of Americans, subjects tended to focus on a specific other person (e.g., "I hoped my sister would have a healthy baby") whereas the Koreans tended to focus on broader personal and social ideals (e.g., "I hoped to be the most humanistic person").

Controllability and probability of attainment. Subjects were asked to rate on 11-point scales whether the hoped-for event could be achieved through personal effort (0) or whether it was determined by situational factors (10). They also rated the probability—when hope first began—of attaining the hoped-for event (0% to 100%). Koreans reported both a greater degree of personal control (3.26 vs 4.55, $F(1,196)$ = 3.79, $p < .05$) and a higher initial probability of attaining the hoped-for event (65.4 % vs 55.4%, $F(1,196)$ = 4.89, $p < .05$). Both of these differences reflect the greater emphasis on individual responsibility that surrounds the Korean conception of hope.

Instrumental responses. What a person does in a situation is, to a certain extent, a function of perceived control. Therefore, subjects were divided into a personal-control group (those scoring below the midpoint of the controllability scale) and a situational-control group (those scoring above the midpoint of the scale). Subjects who scored at the midpoint were eliminated from consideration. The number of subjects in each group and the results of the analyses are presented in Table 4.5.

The results presented in Table 4.5 are consistent with those obtained in Study 1 (see Table 1.4).[6] The most frequently endorsed items by both Americans and Koreans were "worked harder," "became better organized," and "thought more creatively." These results suggest that hope is viewed as motivating in both cultures.

---

[6] The wording of the items in Table 4.5 are abbreviated. Except for negligible differences, the items used to assess instrumental responses during hope were the same as those used in Study 1 (see Table 1.4). There were no statistically significant differences between the American samples in Studies 1 and 3 on any of the items. To facilitate comparison, therefore, the items in Table 4.5 are arranged in the same order as those in Table 1.4.

Table 4.5. Mean ratings[a] of instrumental responses during hope as reported by American and Korean subjects. Results are presented separately for subjects who percieved the outcome to be primarily under personal or situational control.

Variable	Personal Control		Situational Control		F-ratios		
	US (n=53)	Korea (n=67)	US (n=36)	Korea (n=22)	Country	Control	Interaction
Worked harder	1.57	1.43	.83	1.18	.04	25.19**	5.26*
Became better organized	1.30	1.15	.56	1.09	.39	16.40**	9.57**
Thought creatively	1.22	1.47	1.06	1.00	.16	2.82	.63
Took added risks	.89	.81	.53	.64	.04	6.03*	.70
Relaxed efforts; relied on faith	.45	.27	.83	.32	8.95**	5.27*	2.54
Became cautious; played it safe	1.00	1.07	.50	1.08	4.12*	1.66	2.22
Concentrated on other things	.11	.07	.50	.33	.71	5.95*	.21

[a] 0 = not at all, 1 = somewhat, 2 = very much.
*p <.05
**p <.01

Not surprisingly, perceived control over events had significant effects on how people responded when hopeful. Persons who believed they had control over events reported working harder, becoming better organized, and taking more risks than those who believed events to be largely situationally controlled. On the other hand, subjects in the situational-control group, in comparison with those in the personal-control group, tended to relax their efforts and to concentrate on other things (although the latter response was relatively infrequent for all subjects).

Of greater relevance to our present concerns are the significant main effects for country (US vs Korea). Americans were more likely than Koreans to say that they "relaxed their efforts; relied on faith," and Koreans were more likely than Americans to say that they "became cautious; played it safe."

The responses of both groups (relaxing efforts and becoming cautious) represent a kind of disengagement from active coping, but the connotation is obviously quite different. Once again, we see the tendency of Americans to associate hope with faith, especially when personal control is minimal, and of Koreans to rely on internal resources (e.g., intellectual processes).

There also were significant interactions between country and controllability on the two most frequently endorsed variables, "worked harder" and "became better organized." Americans tended to endorse these items primarily when they had some personal control over the outcome. By contrast, degree of personal control had little effect on the responses of the Koreans. These interactions are consistent with the tendency of Koreans to view hope as an aspect of personality rather than as an episodic (situationally controlled) variable.

Discussion: Hope in Cultural Context

To summarize the results of Study 4 briefly, when asked to categorize hope in general, Korean subjects saw hope as a socially acquired but relatively permanent part of personality, closely related to the intellect and will (i.e., a voluntary process). Korean synonyms for hope included such terms as ideal, ambition and effort. Americans, by contrast, categorized hope as a more transitory state—a way of coping, a feeling, and/or an emotion. American synonyms for hope included such terms as faith, prayer, and belief.

When asked to select a representative episode of hope, Koreans (more often than Americans) chose episodes that were of longer duration, that were achievement-related, that involved abstract ideals (with regard to self and society), the attainment of which was more probable and more under personal control. In comparison with the American subjects, however, degree of personal control did not greatly influence the way Koreans said they responded while hoping.

The above results help explain the findings of Boucher (1980) that Koreans do not spontaneously list hope as one of the emotions of their culture. To the extent that Koreans conceive of hope as controllable, voluntary, intellectual, and permanent, their concept of hope is, in important respects, incompatible with the experience of emotion.

It is beyond the scope of the present analysis to explore all the factors—historical and contemporaneous—that might account for the differences in the way hope is conceived and experienced by Americans and Koreans. Our present remarks will be limited to a few observations on the relation of hope to religious/intellectual systems in the United States and Korea.

Traditionally, Americans—even those who profess no religion—have been greatly influenced by the Judeo-Christian religious tradition. That fact requires little documentation. During the past century, Christianity has also become a major religion in Korea, counting among its adherents roughly one quarter of the population (both Protestant and Catholic). However, the Korean national character (whether Christian or nonChristian) has been shaped predominantly by Confucianism, which is as much an intellectual as a religious ideology.[7] In this connection, it is worth quoting Dr. Hyon Sang-yun, a leader of the Korean nationalist movement against the Japanese and subsequently President of Korea University, Seoul. According to Dr. Hyon the influence of Confucianism "on the life and thought of Korean society has been profound. It gave direction to Korean philosophy and character to the nation and it wrought important national changes, politically, culturally, and economically" (quoted by Yi, 1983, p. 113).

One of the major differences between the Judeo-Christian and Confucian intellectual traditions has to do with

---

[7]   Other important influences on Korean culture include Buddhism and Taoism, although their impact, especially in recent history, is generally regarded as weaker than that of Confucianism. However, even if these within cultural differences were taken into account, the nature of our argument would not be weakened. As Ching (1977, p.152) has observed, Buddhism, Taoism, and Hinduism, as well as Confucianism, all emphasize "self-transcendence," "self-exertion," and "striving for inner enlightenment." This contrasts with the major Western religions of Judaism, Christianity, and Islam, which are characterized by faith in a supernatural being.

the place of humans in the broader scheme of things. In the book of Genesis, humans are given dominion "over every living thing that moveth upon the earth." Yet, humans are themselves conceived of as finite creatures who must trust in the ultimate goodness and wisdom of divine providence for their own salvation. The Judeo-Christian tradition is thus action oriented, but not necessarily internally oriented. That is, it encourages action in situations where action is possible, and a reliance on faith in situations of helplessness.

In Confucianism, faith in a transcendental and ultimately benevolent power is less important than is cultivation of one's own humanity or *jen*. "The universal and all-comprehensive norm of conduct is not an external law established by the belief of revelation, but a completely interiorized evaluating mind that should function correctly each time it responds to a new situation" (Chih, 1981, p. 436). The goal of Confucianism is to become a sage. A sage does not act out of the desires of the moment; nor does a sage attempt to impose his or her will on external events. The ideal is harmony—with one's self, with others, and with nature.

The differential influence of hope within the Judeo-Christian and Confucian traditions is evidenced by the fact that hope and its variants (e.g., hoping) is mentioned over 150 times in the Bible (*New American Standard Exhaustive Concordance*), but not once in *The Analects of Confucius*. The latter is a much smaller work, but that does not account for the difference. "Desire," a frequently mentioned synonym of hope by both Americans and Koreans (see Table 4.2), is often referred to in *The Analects of Confucius*, but typically as something to be overcome, or at least to be brought into harmony with the moral order.

> The Master [Confucius] said, at fifteen I set my heart upon learning. At thirty, I had planted my feet firm upon the ground. At forty, I no longer suffered from perplexities. At fifty, I knew what were the biddings of Heaven. At sixty, I heard them with docile ear. At seventy, I could follow the dictates of my own heart; for what I desired no longer overstepped the boundaries of right. (Waley, 1938, 2.4)

In the present study, the possible influence of the Judeo-Christian tradition on American conceptions of hope, and of Confucianism on Korean conceptions, is evident in a variety of ways. For example, "faith" and "prayer" are among the most frequently mentioned synonyms of hope mentioned by Americans, whereas "ideal" and "ambition" are more similar to the Korean conception of hope. Consider, also, the rules of hope. The major rules for Americans focus on whether or not hope is prudent (realistic). By contrast, Koreans tend to adopt a more moralistic outlook when deciding whether it is appropriate to hope. (For example, is the event contrary to personal and/or social values? Does it contribute to the general good?) Both cultures emphasize action rules, but in somewhat different ways. As we have seen, the Western tradition links hope to faith, and to a reliance on God's will (or fate, in more secular versions) as well as on individual effort. Although God presumably helps those most who help themselves, an overreliance on faith clearly threatens the relation between hope and action. This is one reason so many folk sayings and maxims warn against the potentially enervating effects of hope (see Study 3). Koreans, on the other hand, evidently see a more straightforward and unambiguous relation between hope and action. Within the Confucian tradition, there is no beneficent deity to rely upon, only one's internal resources. Hope and action therefore become closely fused; so fused, in fact, that there may be little need for action rules distinct from other rules of hope. Finally, for Koreans in comparison with Americans, hope is not so much a transitory emotional state as it is an integral aspect of one's own personality; and, hence, instrumental responses during hope are relatively independent of the immediate situation (i.e., perceived personal versus situational control).

We do not wish to imply that the Judeo-Christian and Confucian traditions can, by themselves, account for the observed differences between American and Korean conceptions of hope. Japan, like Korea, has been much influenced by Confucianism. Yet, it will be recalled that Boucher (1980) found hope to be among the emotions listed by Japanese informants (but not by informants from Indonesia, Malaysia, and Sri Lanka). Similarly, not all cultures influenced by the Judeo-Christian tradition conceive of hope in exactly the same manner. In Spanish, for example, the same term, *esperanza*, refers to both hope and expectation. This can blur the distinction between emotional and rational grounds when predicting future events (such as grades on an examination, Romero, 1988).

In short, a comprehensive analysis of hope would require comparisons not only between America and Korea, but also among different Western and Eastern societies. Nevertheless, the major point we wish to make does not depend upon such a comprehensive analysis: Hope, like other emotional syndromes, cannot be understood apart from the sociocultural context of which it is a part.

V

Conclusion:
Emotion, Self and Society

In the preceding chapters we have tried to develop a relatively clear and comprehensive picture of hope. To review briefly, Study 1 distinguished hope from want and desire and identified four prototypic rules of hope: prudential rules, priority rules, moralistic rules, and action rules. While there is nothing inherent in these rules that prescribes an emotion, Study 2 showed that, in many important ways, hope conforms to the American understanding of the emotional model: Hope is difficult to control, it affects one's thoughts and actions, it motivates behavior, and it is seen (erroneously, in some respects) as a universal experience. In Study 3, the characteristics of hope identified in the two previous studies were confirmed through an analysis of metaphors and maxims. And finally, the cultural relativity of hope was explored in Study 4.

As was discussed in Chapter 1, we take a social-constructionist view of emotions. In its barest form, this approach sees emotions not as innate reactions but as socially constituted patterns of behavior (including subjective experience). This is not to deny that other factors (e.g., biology and individual development) have a distinct influence on the organization of emotional reactions. Some emotions, of which grief is a good example, appear to be very strongly rooted in our biological heritage—in the case of grief, in the need for affiliation (Averill, 1979; Averill & Nunly, 1988). Grief-like reactions appear in recognizable form in all societies and even in many nonhuman primates. However, even in the case of grief, society plays a major role in determining the final form of the response, as well as many of the specific modes of expression. For other emotions, including hope, a greater range of cross- cultural variation is apparent, indicating that socialization plays a greater part, and biology a lesser part, in their determination.

In order to understand specific emotions, and emotions generally, we have introduced the notion of an emotional model (see Chapter 3). The first part of the present chapter is devoted to a further exploration of the role and nature of the emotional model as exemplified by hope. In subsequent sections, we explore two other questions inherent in the social constructionist perspective: (a) How is hope related to the self? and (b) How is hope related to the society? Stated more colloquially: What does hope do for the individual? And for the group?

The Emotional Model

Any area of inquiry must start with some assumptions about the appropriate unit of analysis. In the study of emotion, three possibilities exist, each legitimate in its own right, but each carrying somewhat different theoretical implications. The three possibilities are (a) emotional syndromes, (b) emotional states, and (c) emotional reactions. An emotional *syndrome* is a theoretical entity; it represents the set of rules and responses that constitute any given emotion. When we speak of hope, anger, love, etc., in the abstract, we are referring to emotional syndromes. An emotional *state* is a temporary (episodic) disposition on the part of an individual to respond in a manner representative of one or another emotional syndrome. An emotional *reaction* is the actual (and highly variable) set of responses manifested by an individual when in an emotional state. We will discuss briefly each of these three types of variables (syndromes, states, and reactions) in reverse order; we will then be in a position to describe more clearly what we mean by an emotional model.

Most traditional theories have tended to emphasize emotional reactions, often identifying emotional states and even syndromes with specific kinds of responses (e.g., expressive reactions, physiological arousal, and/or subjective experience). As Studies 1 and 2 illustrate, such an emphasis on response variables is not tenable in the case of hope. The way hope is experienced and expressed is as varied as the things for which a person might hope and the conditions that may initiate an episode. Similar considerations apply to other emotions, including anger (Averill, 1982) and love (Averill, 1985), but they are especially evident in the case of hope.

For the above reasons, hopeful states can best be conceptualized as episodic dispositions (Averill, in press a). The qualifier, "episodic," helps to distinguish emotional states from other emotionally relevant dispositions, such as temperamental traits. For example, hope (as opposed to an optimistic personality trait–cf. Scheier & Carver, 1985) is a relatively short-term response tendency, usually initiated and terminated by specific environmental conditions. Stated somewhat differently, the person who is hopeful is temporarily disposed to feel and react in ways that conform to the syndrome of hope.

And what, more precisely, is the syndrome of hope? As already noted, an emotional syndrome is not a state of the individual nor a specific set of reactions. Rather, it is a theoretical entity–a representation or meaning imposed on events. Toulmin (1953) has compared scientific theories to maps; with slight modification, we can use the same analogy to explicate the nature of syndromes. When we speak of anger, love, hope, etc., in the abstract, we are drawing a concise verbal map of the kinds of situations and behaviors that tend to occur when the person is in the relevant emotional state. A syndrome, however, is not like an ordinary map, which describes but does not alter the terrain it represents. A syndrome is more like an architect's blueprint—it is a "prescriptive description." The syndrome of hope says that under appropriate circumstances, certain internal and external responses can be assembled to form a coherent structure.

Specific emotional syndromes, such as hope, anger, and love, are closely related to the behavior they represent. As a group, they are also related to a higher-order (more abstract) model that we are calling the emotional model. Like specific syndromes, the emotional model is a theoretical entity, a prescriptive description of a range of behaviors.[1]

In Study 2, a number of the parameters that define a response as an emotion, as opposed to some other form of behavior (e.g., a purposeful or rational act) were identified. Specifically, emotions are understood to be difficult to control, to affect one's thoughts and actions, and to motivate behavior. Responses that fall within the range of these parameters are generally classified as emotional.

To clarify further what we mean by the emotional model, a comparison might be made to the medical model. In both cases the behavior (emotion or disease) is interpreted as a passion (something that happens to the person) rather than as an action, and the individual is accorded certain rights and responsibilities. Of course, there are vital differences between emotional and disease syndromes, the most important of which is that emotions are not organically determined; and while emotions may involve pathos, they are not pathological in the usual sense. But even these differences require instructive qualifications. For example, emotions have often

---

[1] In speaking of *the* emotional model, we are not precluding the possibility that there may be a variety of such models, depending on which parameters of emotion are emphasized. Thus, we will often speak of *an* emotional model, recognizing that not everywhere are emotions conceived similarly. The important point is that the model represents the class of emotions, not just a single emotion.

been treated as "diseases of the mind" (e.g., by the Stoics, Kant). Also, the degree of organic disfunction may vary from one disease to another, being high in cancer, say, and low or nonexistent in functional disorders, such as neurotic or hysterical conversion reactions. In the latter case, the "disease" is constituted by the syndrome as understood by the patient. Conditions such as hysterical conversion reactions might better be—and often are—considered "emotional disorders" rather than diseases per se.

Now let us return to the syndrome of hope. When confronted with the prospect of a desired but uncertain event, people may adopt either an emotional or a nonemotional model. Hope signifies the adoption of an emotional model. What would represent the adoption of a nonemotional model in similar circumstances? We have seen in Study 4 that, for Koreans, *himang* refers to roughly the same kind of experience as does hope, but within a nonemotional framework. In Western societies, optimism is in important respects similar to hope, but without the corresponding emotional connotation. Hence, the contrast between hope and optimism can be used to clarify the nature of the emotional model.

People can be hopeful or optimistic about the same set of circumstances, and they might do much the same thing whether hopeful or optimistic. Nevertheless, there is a clear difference between hope and optimism. To illustrate, consider the difference in connotation between the following two statements: "I hope that the economy will improve"; and "I am optimistic that the economy will improve." A political candidate who expressed hope with regard to the economy would likely inspire less confidence than one who expressed optimism. Why?

We expect claims of optimism to be based on evidence that can be judged in terms of rational criteria. Thus, the more likely an event, the more reason for optimism. Hope, too, should have a reasonable basis (as implied by the prudential rules). However, as the results of Study 1 indicate, a curvilinear relation exists between hope and the probability of an event. We should not hope for events that are either too unlikely or virtually assured. Optimism, by contrast, may increase linearly with the probability of attainment.

Another difference between hope and optimism relates to the importance of the event. If an event is sufficiently important, hope may be considered appropriate even though chances of fulfillment are practically nil. By contrast,. the importance of an event does not, by itself, justify optimism. If the odds are nil, optimism is not warranted even in a life-threatening situation. Thus, a person with presumably incurable cancer might be told: "Though there is little reason for optimism, don't lose hope." This kind of "reality negotiation" (Snyder, 1988) is central to emotional models, and moderate degrees of it are regularly associated with psychological health (Taylor & Brown, 1988).

Hope is also related to a person's value structure differently than is optimism. The range of appropriate objects of hope is tightly curtailed by the moral ideals of the individual and society. As demonstrated in Studies 1 and 4, especially, there are numerous things that people might want but for which they feel they should not hope (material gains, hedonistic pleasures, etc.). Optimism is more (but not completely) neutral in this respect. This helps explain why political candidates are likely to refer to hope when speaking about broad ideals (e.g., a just society) but to optimism when speaking about technical issues. To oversimplify somewhat, hope tells us about the person's values, optimism about the person's assessment of the situation.

From the above comparisons, a picture begins to emerge of the essential differences between an emotional model, as exemplified by hope, and a nonemotional model, as represented by optimism.[2] The parameters and rules of an

---

[2] As described in Chapter 3, there are a variety of nonemotional models. For ease of discussion, we are subsuming optimism under a rational model. However, folk models of behavior are somewhat fuzzy around the edges, and while optimism does not conform to the parameters of the emotional model, neither is it a prime example of rational behavior. Of all the ways of anticipating a future event, the most "objective" is expectancy. An expected event may be either good or bad, personal or impersonal. Optimism, by contrast, implies that the expected event is positive and in some way personally relevant; it also implies a certain hedging or uncertainty with respect to probabilities, but not the abandonment of rational justification. But be that as it may, the very closeness of

emotional model are epitomized by the notion of subjectivity. The emotions are subjective; rational thought, by contrast, is objective. Unfortunately, the notion of subjectivity as applied to the emotions is ambiguous. "Subjectivity" can be interpreted in either of two ways. The first way is exemplified by such statements as, "You can't trust his judgment; he is too subjective." This sense of subjectivity implies a biased, irrational, or even deluded form of judgment. It is what Calhoun (1989) has called *epistemological subjectivity*. Emotions can be subjective in this sense, but as the prudential rules of hope illustrate, that is not normative.

The second sense of subjectivity is illustrated by such statements as, "I find that picture disgusting," or "Your attitude makes me angry." Such statements do not necessarily imply a biased or irrational judgment. They do, however, imply that the instigating conditions are evaluated in relation to the subject's own interests and values. Calhoun (1989) has called this sense, *biographical subjectivity*. Emotions are subjective in this sense, for they place events within the context of the individual's own history and goals.

Calhoun (1989) argues that biographical and not epistemological subjectivity distinguishes emotional from nonemotional states. We agree, but with an important qualification. People are not simply free to "choose" their emotions on the basis of their personal history, interests and values, as Calhoun implies. What is most characteristic about emotions is not their biographical nature, but their *relational* nature. And it is society, more than personal history, that determines the kind of subject-object relations that constitute the various emotions.

Put somewhat differently, the "biographical subjectivity" of emotions is a particularization of a "social intersubjectivity," the latter being a function of the history of the group. This accounts for the fact, frequently noted but seldom explained, that an intellectual knowledge of the norms, rules, and customs of a society (such knowledge as an anthropologist might have) is not sufficient for membership in that society;

hope and optimism makes their differences even more instructive.

of greater importance is the ability to experience the emotions that are meaningful within the society.

The above observations are well illustrated by hope. For hope to be considered "real," it should be prudent, important, moral, and action-oriented. Anything else might be considered a "false" hope. Needless to say, it is society as much as the person that determines what is prudent, important, moral, and warrants action. Indeed, as will be discussed more fully in a subsequent section, under the right circumstances, hope is often considered a *duty*, an obligation of the individual to the group.

Lest it be thought that hope is peculiar in this regard, it might be worthwhile to note the criteria for attributing anger in courts of law. Two of these criteria—the adequacy of provocation and insufficient cooling time—are judged on the basis of the so-called "reasonable man test." This test basically asks: Was the provocation sufficient to arouse an ordinary member of the community to anger? And, again in terms of community standards, was there insufficient time for the anger to dissipate before the act was committed? In answering these questions, the actual state of mind of the individual is irrelevant. A person who does not conform to community standards in these regards cannot be truly angry, regardless of his feelings at the time.

Similar considerations apply to love (Averill, 1985) and other emotions, but we need not belabor the point. To summarize briefly, the interpretation of behavior as emotional implies the application of a particular explanatory model to the behavior in question. The same set of reactions can be interpreted in terms of an emotional or a nonemotional model. We emphasize this point because it is often assumed that the application of different models implies differences in underlying psychological processes. Sometimes that is the case, but it is not a necessary implication. Neither hope nor anger depends on an "emotion system" separate from a more rational "cognitive system," if by "system" we mean a unique set of mechanisms of biological or psychological origin. "Rational" and "emotional" behavior can be understood to be expressions of a single system with a range of capabilities. Emotional behaviors may be less conscious and less subject to logical argument than rational behaviors, but this represents a differences in the way processes are organized and not an essential difference in the processes per se.

One final point before leaving this topic: In the above discussion, we have frequently made reference to the rules of hope, as indicated by the results of Study 1, and the parameters of hope as an emotion, as indicated by the results of Study 2. The parameters (representing the commonalities between hope and other emotions) help define what we mean by an emotional model, whereas the rules help stipulate what a person should or should not do when hopeful. We have made this distinction largely for analytical purposes. As already noted, a close relation exists between the model of hope as an emotion and the rules of hope. Specifically, the model helps determine the rules and the rules help constitute the model. In other words, we are not dealing here with two distinct phenomena, but with a whole-part relation. The distinction is nevertheless important. The whole is not simply the sum of its parts; nor are the parts completely determined by the whole.

These considerations suggest that hope can be fostered in either of two ways: from the top down (a model-based approach) or from the bottom up (a rule-based approach). For example, a person might be encouraged to "keep up hope," thus invoking the general model of hope as an emotion; the application of the rules of hope would then follow. Or, a person might first recognize implicitly that one or more of the rules of hope apply in a situation, and then "conclude" that hope as a whole is appropriate. There is a particular danger in the top-down approach—a person may adopt a hopeful stance in a situation where the rules of hope do not apply. As we saw in Study 3, folk wisdom contains ample warnings against such vain and foolish hopes.

Hope as Related to the Self

Why adopt an emotional as opposed to a nonemotional model? For example, why be hopeful when, on rational grounds, pessimism might be warranted? This question brings us to a consideration of the functional significance of hope, which can be addressed on both an individual and a social level. In this section, we deal with the significance of hope for the individual.

Hope, it has been said, is the best medicine. Many other metaphors analyzed in Study 3 also attest to hope's motivational and life-sustaining qualities. Hope nourishes, guides, uplifts, and supports a person in times of difficulty. This is also a common theme in medical and psychological writings. The patient without hope presumably has a poor prognosis. One of the most fundamental issues with respect to hope is whether this way of talking has any basis in reality, or whether it is merely a reflection of our implicit (but perhaps vacuous) folk model of hope. And if it does have a basis in reality, how might we account for such beneficial effects?

There is mounting empirical evidence that an optimistic outlook may indeed have a beneficial effect on recovery from illness (Scheier & Carver, 1985) and, conversely, that a pessimism may have an adverse effects (Peterson & Seligman, 1987). As noted earlier, very similar—if not the same—behaviors can be labeled hope or optimism, depending on whether one adopts an emotional or a nonemotional model. Hence, what is true of optimism in this regard should also be true of hope. Indeed, since a person can maintain hope even in situations where rational considerations call for pessimism, the beneficial effects of hope should be even more general than those of optimism.

Assuming, then, that hope does in fact have beneficial effects for the individual, how do we account for this fact? Like many issues in psychology, the answer to this question involves both conceptual and empirical considerations. Let us begin with the conceptual. We argued above that an emotional state is not a specific response or "happening" within the body. It is, rather, an episodic disposition, a temporary tendency to respond in conformance with the parameters and rules that help constitute an emotional syndrome. It follows that an emotion cannot cause behavior, at least not in the traditional sense of efficient causation (like one billiard ball hitting another). As episodic dispositions, emotional states are not events at all. Rather, they fall within the category of formal causes. To illustrate by way of analogy, to say that someone "exploded" because of anger is analogous to saying that a material burst into flames because it was (temporarily) in a combustible state. Combustibility is not an event or occurrence, it is a state of the material.

Of course, dispositional (formal cause) explanations do not take us very far. We must account for the existence of the disposition. We have already indicated the direction such an account might take in the case of emotional states. To repeat, the structure of an emotional state depends on the internalization of the parameters and rules that help define the relevant emotional syndrome.

With the above considerations as background, we can now consider briefly the mechanism by which hope might exert its beneficial effects. We will limit our remarks to recovery from illness, for this is illustrative of the more general case of how hope—and emotions in general—can influence or "cause" behavior.

To make our observations concrete, consider the case of a person who is gravely ill, and who has "given up all hope." Through some change in circumstance (see Table 1.2, Study 1), the person suddenly "gains hope" and recovery ensues. How do we account for such a result?

A direct, enhancing effect of hope on immune functioning cannot be ruled out. However, we believe there are other, more simple explanations. For example, the person who gains hope is committed to action, if action is possible (action rules). This might entail, among other things, seeking and following medical advice; eliciting social support; adopting a vigilant orientation, which in turn might increase the chances of successful coping; and the like.

But what if there are no actions to be taken? Sometimes there is nothing a person can do except hope. When no specific action is feasible, hope may still serve as a regulatory principle, lending a "sense of coherence" to experience. Atonovsky (1979) has marshalled evidence from a variety of sources that persons who have a strong sense of coherence in their lives are more resistant to disease than are those who experience life as fractionated and disorganized.

Coherence reflects "a global orientation that expresses the extent to which one has a pervasive, enduring though dynamic feeling of confidence that one's internal and external environments are predictable and that there is a high probability that things will work out as well as can reasonably be expected" (p. 123). Such a global orientation, if based on faith rather than rational considerations, is part of what we mean by hope.

To summarize these considerations briefly, when a person "gains" hope, what is gained is not some mysterious quality, like the active but unknown ingredient of a drug. Rather, what is gained is disposition to think and act in ways consistent with the rules of hope. Specifically, the person who is sincerely and appropriately hopeful views the future with realism based on faith, not Pollyannish denial (prudential rules); regards as important (priority rules) and socially acceptable (moralistic rules) the events hoped for; and within the realm of the possible, is ready to do whatever is necessary to make the future a reality (action rules).

Hope as Related to Society

The emotions are linchpins linking individuals to society. The meaning and significance of an emotion is thus to be found on the social as well as on the individual level of analysis.

In discussing the results of Study 4, we noted how hope qua emotion is related to the Judeo-Christian tradition within Western cultures, whereas *himang* (which is similar in most respect to hope, but is not interpreted within an emotional model) is more closely related to Confucianism. The influence of the Judeo-Christian tradition on hope is as readily apparent today as it is historically. The philosopher Fackenheim (1970) has posed the question: "How come Jews are still around after thousands of years, mostly exiled?" There is only one answer, he maintains, and that is *hope*. According to Fackenheim, hope is a "Jewish duty," now more than ever. "I think merely to survive, to exist as a Jew after Auschwitz, is to be committed to hope: to hope because you are commanded to hope, because to despair would be a sin" (p. 91).

Echoing Fackenheim, the Christian theologian, Moltmann (1980) argues that "hope is a command. Obeying it means life, survival, endurance, standing up to life until death is swallowed up in victory" (p. 20).

Brunner (1956) relates the centrality of hope in Judaism and Christianity to the fact that these (and Mohammedanism, too) are historical religions. That is, they place great emphasis on specific events occurring in the past and, by extension, on events that are promised to happen in the future (e.g., the coming of a messiah, redemption). But hope is not a product of any specific religion, nor is it confined to religious systems in general. Indeed, hope may be "commanded" by any social ideology that promises a better future in spite of the realities of a problematic present. Hope serves to maintain loyalty and commitment without requiring rational justification. The faith on which the hope is based need not be in some divine providence: It could be in the inevitable workings of history, in the progress of science, in the power of some charismatic leader, or whatever.

In view of the above, it should come as no surprise that one of the major contemporary works on hope is by a Marxist philosopher, Ernst Bloch (1959/1986), an avowed atheist. Marxism sees in the dialectics of history the replacement of existing miseries and injustices with a world of material abundance, human equality, and self-fulfillment. And although this will supposedly come to pass through historical necessity, the faithful are nevertheless obliged to take whatever actions are deemed prudent to assist the process.

Hope is also a central ingredient of what Bellah (1967) has called the "civil religion" of the United States. In the early years of the Republic, the United States was often compared by its political leaders with ancient Israel. Europe was Egypt, and America, the promised land. President Kennedy's inaugural address, with its almost biblical ring, provides a recent example of this characteristic of the American political system:

Now the trumpet summons us again—not as a call to bear arms, though arms we need—not as a call to battle, though embattled we are—but as a call to bear the burden of a long twilight struggle, year in and year out, "rejoicing in hope, patient in tribulation"—a struggle against the common enemies of man: tyranny, poverty, disease and war itself. . . . With a good conscience our only sure reward, with history the final judge of our deeds, let us go forth to lead the land we love, asking His Blessing and His help, but knowing that here on earth God's work must truly be our own (quoted by Bellah, p. 4, 5).

We do not wish to imply that hope is a peculiarly Western phenomenon, tied to specific religious and political systems. Hope, or something very closely akin to hope, can be found in a wide variety of messianic and utopian social movements, both religious and secular (Desroche, 1979). The main point we are trying to illustrate is the following: From a social perspective, hope is a command to "keep the faith," to remain loyal and committed to action, secure in one's moral righteousness, even when rational considerations and empirical evidence might call for skepticism. It is a powerful social tool, and it undoubtedly has been independently invented many times in many different places.

Final Observations

Hope is, in the words of Kierkegaard, "the passion for the possible" (cited by Godfrey, 1987, p. 29). We have said enough about what it means for hope to be a passion. Let us conclude with a few words about the possible. For hope to be meaningful in the fullest sense, the possible must take two forms. First, the world itself must consist of possibilities, not necessities. If all were predetermined, then a person could only wait for the inevitable. In that case, hope would be, if not an outright evil as suggested by the myth of Pandora, then at least little more than a defense against pessimism. Second, human nature, too, must consist of possibilities. It has been said that humans are creatures of hope. This does not mean that humans, because of their great cognitive capacities, are the only beings capable of imagining future alternatives. More profoundly, it means that by projecting themselves into the future, people can help create not only their own futures but also their own selves in the process. With hope, we can begin to realize the possibilities inherent both in the situation and in ourselves.

Appendix

Questionnaire Used in Studies 1 and 2

Hope has frequently been referred to as one of the most characteristic and essential features of human nature; it has also been regarded as superficial, misleading, and illusory–like an awakened dream. There has been, however, little research on which to base a comprehensive analysis of hope.

This is one of a series of studies designed to explore some of the ways in which hope is experienced in everyday contexts. The study involves a detailed questionnaire on your experiences of hope. Many of the questions can be answered simply by placing a check next to an appropriate item, or by circling a number which best describes your experiences. Thus, although the questionnaire may appear lengthy, it is easy to complete within an hour.

There are no right or wrong answers to any of the items in the questionnaire. People differ widely in what they hope for, and how they respond when hoping. Therefore, let your own experiences determine how you answer the questions. Please be perfectly frank, and <u>be sure to answer all of the items</u>, otherwise your questionnaire may be useless. Your answers will be completely anonymous; at no point are you asked to identify yourself personally on the questionnaire.

Most people have found the questionnaire interesting to complete, and we believe you will too. Thank you for your assistance.

1. To begin, think of something that your presently <u>want</u> or <u>desire</u> very much, but that you do <u>not</u> hope for.

_____
_____
_____

2. Now think of something that you not only want, but also hope for.

_____
_____
_____

3. What features do you think are present in the second situation (#2) that are not present in the first situation (#1), such that in the second you are hoping whereas in the first you are only wanting?

_____
_____
_____

4. Try to recall how often you experienced hope during the last week. If you hoped repeatedly for the same thing (e.g., all week you were hoping to pass an exam), count that as one episode. In your answer, <u>be sure to distinguish between hoping for something and simply wanting or desiring something</u>.

Before answering this question, think back through each day of the week, then indicated how many times (in total) you hoped for something.

_____ not at all
_____ 1 to 2 times per week
_____ 3 to 5 times per week
_____ 1 time per day
_____ 2 to 3 times per day
_____ 4 to 5 times per day
_____ 6 to 10 times per day
_____ more than 10 times per day

The following questions (5-24) all pertain to one episode of hope. The episode should have the following characteristics: (a) it both started and ended within the past year; (b) it represents hope, not simply want or desire

To pick an appropriate episode, think back over the entire year. During that time, you undoubtedly started hoping for something that you did not hope for before, and that you are not currently hoping for. Choose one such incident that you believe best represents hope. (Note: If you did not experience an episode during the year that you believe clearly represents hope, then pick the most recent incident before that.)

Before answering the following questions, think carefully about the episode you have chosen, and try to relive your experiences as they happened at the time.

5. Please describe what you hoped for:

_____
_____
_____

6. Was the event you hoped for something that was under your control (e.g., that you could obtain through your own

efforts)?   Or was it something that was determined by factors beyond your control (e.g., up to chance or fate)?

completely due   completely due to
factors   0   1   2   3   4   5   6   7   8   9   10   factors
under your   beyond your
control   control

7.   When did you start hoping for this event?   (give month and year)

_____   _____
month   year

8.   How long did your hope last?

_____   1 day or less
_____   1 week or less
_____   1 month or less
_____   3 months or less
_____   6 months or less
_____   1 year or less
_____   less than 1 year

No matter how long your episode of hope lasted, you may distinguish three points in time: (a) the beginning, just after you started hoping; (b) the middle, about half way through the episode; (c) the end, just before you stopped hoping.   Answer the following questions with respect to each point in time.

9.   What did you believe the chances were that your hope would be fulfilled?

a.   at the beginning, just after you started hoping:

0% 10% 20% 30% 40% 50% 60% 70% 80% 90% 100%
no chance   certain
that it would   that it would
be fulfilled   be fulfilled

b.   at the mid-point, about half-way through the episode:

 0% 10% 20% 30% 40% 50% 60% 70% 80% 90% 100%
no chance   certain
that it would   that it would
be fulfilled   be fulfilled

c.   at the end, just before you stopped hoping:

 0% 10% 20% 30% 40% 50% 60% 70% 80% 90% 100%
no chance   certain
that it would   that it would
be fulfilled   be fulfilled

10.   How intense was your hope?

a.   at the beginning, just after you started hoping:

not at all   0   1   2   3   4   5   6   7   8   9   10   very
intense   intense

b.   at the mid-point, about half-way through the episode:

not at all   0   1   2   3   4   5   6   7   8   9   10   very
intense   intense

c.   at the end, just before you stopped hoping:

not at all   0   1   2   3   4   5   6   7   8   9   10   very
intense   intense

11.   How important did you consider the event that you hoped for?

a.   at the beginning, just after you started hoping, you considered the event:

not at all   0   1   2   3   4   5   6   7   8   9   10   very
important   important

b.   at the mid-point, about half-way through the episode, you considered the event:

not at all   <u>0</u> <u>1</u> <u>2</u> <u>3</u> <u>4</u> <u>5</u> <u>6</u> <u>7</u> <u>8</u> <u>9</u> <u>10</u>   very
important   important

c.   at the end, just before you stopped hoping, you considered the event:

not at all   <u>0</u> <u>1</u> <u>2</u> <u>3</u> <u>4</u> <u>5</u> <u>6</u> <u>7</u> <u>8</u> <u>9</u> <u>10</u>   very
important   important

12.   The following items describe various ways you may have felt before you started hoping, and the kinds of incidents or changes that sometimes initiate hope.   Check the item that best describes the change in circumstances that made you first start hoping.

_____ a.   I had not thought about the event before; it represented a new possibility for me.

_____ b.   The event seemed very unlikely; but then the chances increased, and so I started to hope.

_____ c.   I was confident that the event would occur; but then I realized it was not certain, and so I started to hope.

_____ d.   The event seemed unimportant to me; but then I came to realize how important it actually was.

_____ e.   The event seemed far in the future; there was time to worry about it later.   But as the event grew closer (became more imminent), I started to hope.

_____ f.   Other (please specify) _____

13.   In your own words, describe the change in circumstances that made you start hoping for the event.

_____

_____

_____

_____

14. How did you feel about the event <u>before</u> you started hoping? (Circle the appropriate number following each item.)

		not at all	somewhat	very much
a.	indifferent, not caring	0	+1	+2
b.	good, pleased, glad	0	+1	+2
c.	irritable, hostile, aggravated	0	+1	+2
d.	confident, assured, optimistic	0	+1	+2
e.	depressed, unhappy, sad	0	+1	+2
f.	ashamed, embarrassed, guilty	0	+1	+2
g.	relieved, calm, satisfied	0	+1	+2
h.	restless, tense, aroused	0	+1	+2
i.	discouraged, let down, disappointed	0	+1	+2
j.	uncertain, confused, bewildered	0	+1	+2
k.	helpless, powerless, lacking in control	0	+1	+2
l.	anxious, nervous, apprehensive about the future	0	+1	+2
m.	other (please specify)_____	0	+1	+2

15.   How did you feel about the event <u>after</u> you started hoping?

		not at all	somewhat	very much
a.	indifferent, not caring	0	+1	+2
b.	good, pleased, glad	0	+1	+2
c.	irritable, hostile, aggravated	0	+1	+2
d.	confident, assured, optimistic	0	+1	+2
e.	depressed, unhappy, sad	0	+1	+2
f.	ashamed, embarrassed, guilty	0	+1	+2
g.	relieved, calm, satisfied	0	+1	+2
h.	restless, tense, aroused	0	+1	+2
i.	discouraged, let down, disappointed	0	+1	+2
j.	uncertain, confused, bewildered	0	+1	+2
k.	helpless, powerless, lacking in control	0	+1	+2
l.	anxious, nervous, apprehensive about the future	0	+1	+2
m.	other (please specify)_____	0	+1	+2

---

16.   At the time when you first started hoping, how easy would it have been for you to give up hope if someone had asked you to?

very   0   1   2   3   4   5   6   7   8   9   10   practically
easy   impossible

17.   The following question is hypothetical and may be difficult to answer.   But try to imagine wanting the event as much as you did, but not hoping for it.   Compared to simply wanting or desiring the event, in what ways do you think you acted differently because of your hope?   Use the following items to make your comparisons:

Because of my hope:	not at all	somewhat	very much
a. I worked harder; was persistent in my efforts	0	+1	+2
b. I relaxed my efforts, relied on faith	0	+1	+2
c. I became better organized; got my act together	0	+1	+2
d. I took added risks; stuck my neck out	0	+1	+2
e. I became cautious; played it safe	0	+1	+2
f. I thought about the issue in a more imaginative and creative way	0	+1	+2
g. I put the issue out of my mind; started to concentrate on other things	0	+1	+2
h. Other (please specify)	0	+1	+2

18. Please explain your response:

_____

_____

_____

The following questions pertain to the termination or end of the episode you have been describing.

19. What change in circumstances made you stop hoping? (Check the item that best describes the change.)

_____ a. I obtained what I was hoping for.

_____ b. The time passed when the event I was hoping for could have occurred, and it didn't.

_____ c. I decided there was little chance of obtaining what I was hoping for (although it was still possible).

_____ d. I came to realize that what I was hoping for was completely under my own control; that is, I could make it happen.

_____ e. I no longer wanted what I had been hoping for.

_____ f. Other (please specify) _____

_____

20. In your own words, describe the changes in circumstance that made you stop hoping for the event.

_____
_____

21. How often does some aspect of the episode presently come to mind?
_____ never   _____ sometimes   _____ frequently

22. Do you presently feel any lingering wish or desire that things would have turned out differently (whether or not you obtained what you hoped for)?

No, things 0 1 2 3 4 5 6 7 8 9 10 Yes,
turned out   I wish things had
for the best   turned out differently

23. Looking back, how do you presently feel about this episode of hoping? That is, are you now indifferent, amused, embarrassed, etc., about this episode?

	not at all	somewhat	very much
indifferent	0	+1	+2
amused	0	+1	+2
embarrassed	0	+1	+2
proud	0	+1	+2
ambivalent	0	+1	+2
dissatisfied with yourself	0	+1	+2
satisfied with yourself	0	+1	+2

other

---

24. Everything considered (the event, what you did and how you felt while hoping, the consequences), do you believe your hope was largely detrimental (worse than useless), neutral, or beneficial.

-3	-2	-1	0	+1	+2	+3
detrimental			neutral			beneficial

25. Please explain: _____

_____

_____

For the next three questions (25-27), think of something that might make your life easier or more enjoyable, but that you do not believe you should hope for.

25. Describe the event:

_____

_____

_____

26. Why do you not hope for it? (Read through the following list; then go back and check each item that applies).

_____ a. The event is unrealistic (can't happen); hope would be an illusion.

_____ b. The event is easily achieved; there is no need to hope.

_____ c. The event is trivial or unimportant; it is not worth hoping for.

_____ d. The event is socially unacceptable or inappropriate (e.g., because it is too materialistic, selfish,   or immoral); it would not be right to hope for it.

_____ e. The event is impractical or disadvantageous at the present time (e.g., because it would interfere with other goals, or involve too much or responsibility); it would be unwise to hope for it.

_____ f. Only hard work will achieve the event; hope itself would not help.

_____ g. The event will or will not occur, regardless of your efforts (it is up to fate); hope will not make any difference.

_____ h. Other (please specify) _____

_____

27. In your own words, please explain why you do not hope for the event, even though it would make your life easier or more enjoyable.

_____
_____
_____
_____

28.   This last question concerns the relationship between hope and emotional states in general. Think for a moment about two commonly recognized emotions, such as anger and love. What do they have in common, such that they are both classified as emotions? Now, compare hope with anger and love (not separately, but in terms of their common features).

List two ways in which hope is similar to anger and love.

I. _____
_____
_____

II. _____
_____
_____

List two ways in which hope is different from anger and love.

I. _____
_____
_____

II. _____
_____
_____

Thank you for your assistance.

References

Antonovsky, A. (1979). *Health, stress, and coping.* San Francisco: Jossey-Bass.

Aquinas, T. (1967). *Summa theologiae. Vol. 19. The emotions* (1a2ae 22-30) (Blackfriars). New York: McGraw-Hill.

Aristotle. (1941). *Categories.* In R. McKeon (Ed.), *The basic works of Aristotle* (Oxford Translation). New York: Random House.

Arnold, B. (1960). *Emotion and personality* (2 vols.). New York: Columbia University Press.

Averill, J. R. (1975). A semantic atlas of emotional concepts. *JSAS Catalog of Selected Documents in Psychology, 5,* 330. (Ms. No. 421)

Averill, J. R. (1979). The functions of grief. In C. Izard (Ed.), *Emotions in personality and psychopathology* (pp. 339-368). New York: Plenum.

Averill, J. R. (1980a). A constructivist view of emotion. In R. Plutchik & H. Kellerman (Eds.), *Theories of emotion* (pp. 305-340). New York: Academic Press.

Averill, J. R. (1980b). On the paucity of positive emotions. In K.R. Blankstein, P. Pliner, & J. Polivy (Eds.), *Assessment and modification of emotional behavior* (pp. 7-45). New York: Plenum Press.

Averill, J. R. (1982). *Anger and aggression: An essay on emotion.* New York: Springer-Verlag.

Averill, J. R. (1985). The social construction of emotion: With special reference to love. In K.J. Gergen & K.E. Davis (Eds.), *The social construction of the person.* (pp. 89-109). New York: Springer-Verlag.

Averill, J. R. (in press a). Emotions as episodic dispositions, cognitive schemas, and transitory social roles: Steps toward an integrated theory of emotion. In A. J. Stewart, D. Ozer, & R. Hogan (Eds.), *Perspectives in personality.* Vol. 3. Greenwich, Conn.: JAI Press.

Averill, J. R. (in press b). Inner feelings, works of the flesh, the beast within, diseases of the mind, driving force, and putting on a show: Six metaphors of emotion and their theoretical extensions. In D. Leary (Ed.), *Metaphor in the history of psychology.* Cambridge: Cambridge University Press.

Averill, J. R., & Nunley, E. P. (1988). Grief as an emotion and as a disease. *Journal of Social Issues, 44,* 79-95.

Bellah, R. (1967). Civil religion in America. *Daedalus, 96,* 1-21.

Berger, P., & Luckmann, T. (1966). *The social construction of reality.* Garden City, NY: Doubleday.

Bloch, E. (1986). *The principle of hope* (3 Vols.) (N. Plaice, S. Plaice, & P. Knight, Trans.). Cambridge, MA: MIT Press. (Original work published 1959)

Boucher, J. D. (1980). *Emotion and culture project: Lexicon and taxonomy report.* Unpublished manuscript. Honolulu: East-West Center.

Buck, R. (1985).   Prime theory: An integrated view of motivation and emotion. *Psychological Review, 92,* 389-413.

Breznitz, S. (1986). The effect of hope on coping with stress. In M. H. Appley & R. Trumbull (Eds.), *Dynamics of Stress* (pp. 295-306). New York: Plenum.

Brunner, H. E. (1956). *Faith, hope, and love.* Philadelphia: Westminster Press.

Calhoun, C. (1989). Subjectivity and emotion. *Philosophical Forum, 20,* 195-210.

Capps, W. H. (1970). Mapping the hope movement. In W. H. Capps (Ed.), *The future of hope* (pp. 1-49). Philadelphia: Fortress Press.

Chih, A. (1981).   *Chinese humanism: A religion beyond religion.* Teipei: Fu Jen Catholic University Press.

Ching, J. (1977).   *Confucianism and Christianity.* Tokyo: Kodansha International.

Chomsky, N. (1980). *Rules and representations.* New York: Columbia University Press.

Desroche, H. (1979).   *The sociology of hope* (C. Martin Sperry, Trans.).   London: Routledge & Kegan Paul.

Ekman, P. (1984). Expression and the nature of emotion. In K. Scherer & P. Ekman (Eds.), *Approaches to emotion* (pp. 319-343).   Hillsdale, NJ: Lawrence Erlbaum.

Fackenheim, E. L. (1970). The commandment to hope: A response to eontemporary Jewish experience. In W. H.

124 RULES OF HOPE

Capps (Ed.), *The future of hope* (pp. 68- 91). Philadelphia: Fortress Press.

Fehr, B., & Russell, J. A. (1984). Concept of emotion viewed from a prototype perspective. *Journal of Experimental Psychology: General, 113,* 464-486.

Fischoff, B. (1975). Hindsight =/= forsight: The effect of outcome knowledge on judgment under uncertainty. *Journal of Experimental Psychology: Human Perception and Performance, 1,* 288-299.

Frank, J. D. (1973). *Persuasion and healing* (rev. ed.). Baltimore: Johns Hopkins University Press.

Friedman, S. B., Chodoff, P., Mason, J. W., & Hamburg, D. A. (1963). Behavioral observations on parents anticipating the death of a child. *Pediatrics, 32,* 610-625.

Frijda, N. H. (1986). *The emotions.* Cambridge: Cambridge University Press.

Fromm, E. (1968). *The revolution of hope: Toward a humanized technology.* New York: Harper & Row.

Gentner, D., & Grudin, J. (1985). The evolution of mental metaphors in psychology: A 90-year retrospective. *American Psychologist, 40,* 181- 192.

Godfrey, J. J. (1987). *A philosophy of human hope.* Dordrecht: Martinus Nijhoff.

Gottschalk, L. A. (1974). A hope scale applicable to verbal samples. *Archives of General Psychiatry, 30,* 779-785.

Harré, R. (1983). *Personal being.* Oxford: Basil Blackwell.

Hartley, D. (1966). *Observations on man.* Gainesville, Fla: Scholars Facsimiles & Reprints. (Original work published 1749)

Hume, D. (1888). *Treatise of human nature. Book II* (L. A. Selby-Bigge, Ed.). Oxford: Clarendon Press. (Original work published 1739)

Izard, C. E. (1977). *Human emotions.* New York: Plenum Press.

Johnson-Laird, P. N., & Oakley, K. (1989). The language of emotions: An anlysis of a semantic field. *Cognition and Emotion, 3,* 81-123.

Kant, I. (1966). *Critique of pure reason* (F. M. Muller, Trans.). Garden City, NY: Doubleday. (Original work published 1781)

Kant, I. (1978). *Anthropology from a pragmatic point of view* (V. L. Dowdell, Trans.). Carbondale, Ill: Southern Illinois University Press. (Original work published 1798)

Kovecses, Z. (1986). *Metaphors of anger, pride, and love: A lexical approach to the structure of concepts.* Amsterdam: John Benjamins.

Kovecses, Z. (1988). *The language of love: The semantics of passion in conversational English.* Lewisburg, PA: Bucknell University Press.

Lakoff, G., & Kovecses, Z. (1983). The cognitive model of anger inherent   in American English. *Berkeley Cognitive Science Report No. 10.* University of California, Berkeley.

Lynch, W. F. (1965). *Images of hope.* Notre Dame: University of Notre Dame Press.

Mandler, G. (1984). *Mind and body: Psychology of emotion and stress.* New York: Norton.

Marcel, G. (1962). *Homo viator: Introduction to a metaphysics of hope* (Emma Craufurd, Trans.). New York: Harper Torchbooks.

Matlin, M. W., & Stang, D. J. (1978). *The pollyanna principle*. Cambridge, MA: Schenkman.

Menninger, K. A. (1959). Hope. *American Journal of Psychiatry, 116*, 481-491.

Moltmann, J. (1980). *Experiences of God* (M. Kohl, Trans). Philadelphia: Fortress press.

Myres, J. L. (1949). Elpis. *Classical Review, 63*, 46.

Nietzsche, F. (n.d.). *Thus spake Zarathrustra* (T. Common, Trans.). New York: The Modern Library. (Original work published 1883-84)

Nietzsche, F. (1986). *Human, all too human.* Vol. 1. (R. J. Hollingdale, Trans.). Cambridge: Cambridge University Press. (Original work published 1878)

Peterson, C., & Seligman, M. E. P. (1987). Explanatory style and illness. *Journal of Personality, 55*, 237-265.

Plato. (1961). *Timaeus.* In E. Hamilton & H. Cairns (Eds.), *The collected dialogues of Plato* (pp. 1151-1211). New York: Pantheon Books.

Romero, M. (1988). *Hope and outcome anticipation.* Unpublished Ph.D. dissertation, University of Massachusetts, Amherst, 1988.

Sartre, J. P. (1948). *The emotions: Outline of a theory* (B. Frechtman, trans.). New York: Philosophical Library.

Schachter, S. (1971). *Emotion, obesity, and crime.* New York: Academic Press.

Scheier, M. F., & Carver, C. S. (1985) Optimism, coping, and health: Assessment and implications of generalized outcome expectancies. *Health Psychology, 4*, 219-247.

Shaver, P., Schwartz, J., Kirson, D., & O'Conner, C. (1987). Emotion Knowledge: Further exploration of a prototype approach. *Journal of Personality and Social Psychology, 52,* 1061-1086.

Snyder, C. R. (1989). Reality negotiation: From excuses to hope and beyond. *Journal of Social and Clinical Psychology, 8,* 130-157.

Solomon, R.C. (1976). *The passions.* Garden City, New York: Doubleday Anchor.

Spence, D. P., Scarborough, H. S., & Ginsberg, E. (1978). Lexical correlates of cervical cancer. *Social Science and Medicine, 12,* 141-145.

Storm, C., & Storm T. (1987). A taxonomic Study of the vocabulary of emotions. *Journal of Personality and Social Psychology, 53,* 805-816.

Stotland, E. (1969). *The psychology of hope.* San Francisco: Jossey-Bass.

Taylor, S. E., & Brown, J. D. (1988). Illusion and well-being: A social psychological perspective on mental health. *Psychological Bulletin, 103,* 193-210.

Tomkins, S. S. (1981). The role of facial response in the experience of emotion: A reply to Tourangeau and Ellsworth. *Journal of Personality and Social Psychology, 40,* 355-357.

Toulmin, S. (1953). *The philosophy of science.* New York: Harper Torchbooks.

Tiger, L. (1979). *Optimism: The biology of hope.* New York: Simon and Schuster.

Waley, A. (1938). *The analects of Confucius.* New York: Vintage Books.

Yi, S. U. (1983).   On the criticism of Confucianism in Korea. In Korean National Commission for UNESCO (Eds.), *Main currents of Korean thought* (pp. 112-146).   Seoul: Si-sa-yong-o-sa Publishers.

Author Index

Subject Index

DATE DUE

HIGHSMITH   # 45220